The
T⊚tal
Marriage
Makeover

CONTENTS

A PROVEN PLAN TO REVOLUTIONIZE YOUR MARRIAGE

The T⊕tal Marriage Makeover

David Clarke, PhD

BARBOUR
PUBLISHING

Member of the
Evangelical Christian
Publishers Association

Printed in the United States of America.
5 4 3 2 1

It's Time for Your Marriage Makeover

Stan and Lisa, a newly married couple, bought their first house. It was beautiful, brand-new construction, and everything was just what they wanted. They were thrilled. They moved in and set up housekeeping. The trouble was, neither of them had any idea how to take care of a home. Their parents had taught them zilch about the kind of regular maintenance needed to keep a family home in good working condition. They vacuumed the carpet, dusted, and did superficial cleaning each week. But not knowing any better, they neglected the major areas of upkeep.

As the years rolled on, they added a few kids and life got busier. Time spent chasing the kids around meant even less time for home maintenance. The house got shabbier and more rundown each year. Sure, they noticed some of the house's problems, but because they were still fairly comfortable—and didn't know how to fix anything anyway—they did nothing.

Finally, however, they could no longer ignore the deterioration of their house. The floor shifted when they walked, the paint was peeling inside and out, the plumbing was backed up in the hall bathroom, the front porch was sagging dangerously, and the bricks on the south side of the house were coming loose. When part of the roof fell off during breakfast one day, they realized their house had broken down.

They didn't know how it had happened, and they really had no clue how to fix it. All they knew was that their once beautiful house was in a pitiful state of disrepair. It was no longer livable, and they had to do something about it. They made a few calls to friends and family and found a contractor. He had a good reputation and had renovated many other homes successfully. He assessed their house carefully and told them their home needed a makeover.

He explained how the building had broken down and presented a specific renovation plan. He said that if they followed his makeover strategy, two important things would happen. First, their house would be completely fixed and in better shape than when they bought it. Second, they would know how to keep it in great condition for the rest of their lives.

THE STORY OF YOUR MARRIAGE

I've just told the story of your marriage, haven't I? It's also the story of my own marriage, and the story of just about every couple's marriage. Just like Stan and Lisa's house, your marriage has broken down, and you're finally noticing it. As with Stan and Lisa, it's really nobody's fault. You've done the best you knew how, and it won't do any good to blame your partner. No one warned you that your marriage would go through a breakdown. You had no clear idea what was going on.

YOU NEED A CONTRACTOR

Like the couple with the broken-down house, you know your marriage needs help, but you don't know what to do about it. I do. I know how marriages break down, and I know how to fix them. Renovating marriages is what I do for a living. I've been doing it successfully for more than twenty years.

Think of me as your contractor, but remember that God is the architect. The Marriage Makeover is based on blueprints that God has shown me through Scripture, the couples I've counseled, and my own marriage. I'd love to take credit for the plans, but I can't. They're God's plans. That's why they work.

THE MARRIAGE MAKEOVER

The Marriage Makeover includes fifteen Marriage Makeover Achievements. The first two are key building blocks that prepare you for the entire process. The next twelve are biblical instructions for husbands and wives. The final Achievement is learning conflict resolution skills.

The makeover process begins with two foundational steps. First, *create a support team*. No couple can renovate their marriage by themselves. You need accountability and encouragement from some key individuals. Second, *establish regular couple times*. Without time to communicate, there can be no connection—and thus no positive change. You will use these daily couple times to discuss and apply the major makeover instructions.

The Marriage Makeover blueprint—the real meat of

the book—is contained in chapters 4 through 18. These chapters set forth in clear, practical language God's building instructions for husbands and wives. By doing what God wants you to do as a husband or wife, you will find out how to meet your spouse's deepest needs. By meeting these needs, you will transform your marriage into the relationship that God wants it to be.

Actually, God will do the transforming. As Paul writes, "I can do all things through Him who strengthens me" (Philippians 4:13). You will simply be following God's long-established blueprint for marital success.

God's Marriage Makeover strategy is based on meeting your spouse's needs. Marriages break down when needs go unmet. Therefore, the blueprint for new, improved marriages involves meeting needs. Men, when you carry out God's biblical instructions for husbands, your wife's needs will be met. Women, when you carry out God's biblical instructions for wives, your husband's needs will be met. Your Marriage Makeover will happen naturally as these needs are met. As you continue to meet your spouse's needs, your marriage will remain intimate and strong, and your love for one another will keep growing.

To highlight the impact of the makeover process, I will use letters called "Snapshots." In these letters, one at the end of each chapter, husbands and wives describe how the Marriage Makeover Achievements revolutionized their relationships.

At the end of each chapter, you will also find specific

Makeover Steps to help you put into action what you have learned.

I highly recommend that you read this book together with your spouse and work as a team in applying the makeover strategy. Doing it together will be fun and will also be the most effective way to change your marriage.

If, however, your spouse refuses to join you in reading the book, go ahead and complete it on your own. If you follow the plan, your marriage will still be improved. It will take longer, but it can still lead to a Total Marriage Makeover.

Realization:
"I've been a dummy."
—George

What went wrong?
- George has been selfish.
- George has been lazy.
- George has pushed Donna away.
- George has assumed Donna would "just put up with it."

Current challenges:
- Donna has inner hurts.
- Donna has a lack of trust.

Next steps:
George: Say "I'm sorry"—then prove it with change.
Donna: Join George in reading and applying *The Total Marriage Makeover*.

1. Honestly evaluate your marriage. On a scale from one to ten (one being the brink of divorce and ten being fantastic), where is your marriage? What are the strengths in your marriage, and what are the weaknesses? Be specific.

2. Commit now to each other to follow the Marriage Makeover strategy. Hold hands and pray—out loud—that you will follow through on all the Makeover Steps. Ask God to give you the courage and the tenacity and the compassion to do it.

Chapter 1
The Promise

WHAT KIND OF MARRIAGE ARE YOU IN?

As a clinical psychologist who has been seeing couples in therapy for more than twenty years, I've discovered that all marriages fall into one of five categories: the *Pretty Good Marriage*, the *Dead Marriage*, the *"I Want a Divorce" Marriage*, the *New Marriage*, and the *Great Marriage*. As you read the following real-life stories, I'm certain you'll have no trouble identifying the kind of marriage you and your spouse are in.

The Pretty Good Marriage
Sue glanced briefly at her husband and told me, "Dave, we're here in your office because we've lost our passion and our intimacy. Back in our dating days and for the first few years of marriage, we were so close. We couldn't wait to see each other. We could talk about anything and thoroughly enjoyed our conversations. We were genuinely interested in what was happening in each other's lives. Whatever we did together was great: cuddling in

the family room, sitting in a restaurant, walking in the mall, talking on the phone during the day, making love.

"But in the last several years, things have changed between us. The anticipation and excitement we used to have is gone. That spark, that chemistry, that feeling of being one, isn't there anymore. We still love each other, but it's not the same love. We're content. We're comfortable. We're fine. But not deeply, passionately in love.

"Looking back, I'd say our marriage began to change about seven or eight years after the wedding. Tony was focused on his career, and I was caught up in the kids, my job, and taking care of the home. Nothing bad happened. Our jobs were going well. The kids were healthy, and we loved having a family. We found a great church and got involved there. But life had settled into a routine. It was predictable. We were in a rut, doing the same old things the same old ways.

"We don't spend as much time together, just the two of us. And when we do, it isn't the same. We've lost our special connection. Romance only happens occasionally. We are parents more than we are lovers. We still have sex fairly regularly, but it's kind of a chore. We're meeting a biological need, not expressing passionate love.

"Our marriage is okay. We're solid, stable, and still committed to each other. We'd never even think of getting a divorce. But living without passion and intimacy is no fun. We're afraid if we keep going like this, things will get worse. We're not okay with an okay marriage.

We had a great marriage for a while, and we want that back. Can you help us?"

This couple has the classic Pretty Good Marriage. It's not great. It's not terrible. It's just pretty good. Instead of an amazing, awesome, Fourth of July fireworks show, they settle for a couple of sparklers. Instead of a sleek, beautiful race car, they settle for an old mule pulling a rickety cart.

> Don't mark time in a passive, ho-hum, assembly-line marriage when you can live an adventure as lovers.

The Pretty Good Marriage is unsatisfying, draining, and frankly—boring. If you're in a marriage like this, you know that your level of excitement is hovering near zero. It's nice to be content, comfortable, and stable, but is that really why you got married? You're not even close to the love relationship that God has planned for you. Your Pretty Good Marriage will also not stay pretty good for long. No marriage ever stays the same. Your marriage is either getting better or getting worse. Without some key changes, your Pretty Good Marriage will become a pretty bad marriage, and it won't take long.

The Dead Marriage

As his wife struggled to hold back her tears, John delivered the eulogy for their dead marriage. "I won't lie to you, Dave, our marriage is in bad shape. We've both been unhappy—

miserable, really—for a number of years. The love is gone. We care about each other, but we don't feel love—at least not the way two married persons ought to feel about each other. We're roommates, and that's about it.

"We spend almost no time together. I guess you could say we're living separate lives. I do my thing and she does hers. In the evenings, I watch television or use the computer, and she reads or talks on the phone. We don't talk much, and when we do, it's just about the kids, schedules, business matters, social events, and the weather.

"Romance is only a memory. We don't go out on dates. We eat out on special occasions, but we're only going through the motions. We haven't had sex in quite a while. We're closer to our friends than we are to each other. You've seen those pathetic couples in restaurants who sit there and say nothing to each other? That's us, Doc.

"I think we've given up hope that we can be happy, but we're hanging in there because it's the right thing to do. We're Christians, and we don't want to disobey God by getting a divorce. Plus, we don't want to hurt our kids.

"No one really knows how bad we're doing as a couple. Our friends and family would be shocked to hear what I'm telling you. We figured it couldn't hurt to come in and find out what you think. Is there any hope for us to have a better marriage?"

It doesn't take a clinical psychologist to realize that this is a Dead Marriage. The flame is out; in fact, there aren't even any logs in the fireplace. Their home is a very cold, sad, and unhappy place. They have no emotional, spiritual, or physical connection. It has been so long since they felt any love, or even had a decent conversation, that they don't know where to start.

Those of you in Dead Marriages have almost forgotten what it was like to be happy together. It feels as if your marriage is over and yet you still live together. You have adjusted to this terrible, loveless reality and are trying desperately to make it to the end of the road. It has become an endurance contest, with the two of you hanging side by side at the edge of a cliff. Who will let go first?

God wants you to stay married, but not like this.

The "I Want a Divorce" Marriage

I take one look at this couple and know what's coming. Their marriage is not merely dead; it's done. The spouse who wants out has come in, not for therapy but to tell a Christian psychologist his or her reasons for getting a divorce. It's the same list of pitiful excuses I've heard hundreds of times: I don't love you anymore. *I don't think I ever loved you.* I shouldn't have married you. *We were so young when we got married.* We're two very different persons. *I feel trapped.* We've grown apart. *I've grown beyond you.* This is my one chance for happiness, and I'm taking it. *God's okay with this because He wants me to be happy.* If I love you at all, I'm not *in love* with you. *It's not you; it's me.* I need to find myself. *I'm no good for you.* The kids will be better off because our rotten marriage is hurting them.

Rationalizations. Justifications. Outright lies. The trouble is, this spouse believes every single one of them. In the distorted, sin-fueled mind of the spouse who wants out, it's an airtight case for divorce.

It's very likely that bad, sinful things have happened in the "I Want a Divorce" Marriage: adultery, pornography, alcoholism, drug abuse, workaholism, verbal abuse, physical violence, extreme selfishness, lying, financial mismanagement, a raging temper—you name it. Sometimes one spouse has been a big-time sinner. Sometimes both have. Often one spouse wants out and the other spouse is devastated and wants to save the marriage. Sometimes both spouses want out.

Whatever the particular scenario, the "I Want a Divorce" Marriage is extremely painful. It is an acute crisis, and stress levels are skyrocketing. Humanly speaking, there is no hope. The spouse who wants out isn't kidding. He or she has decided to get a divorce. Without a miracle and aggressive intervention, there will be a divorce.

The New Marriage

The young couple settled on my couch, and the wife spoke: "We've been married a year and a half, and for the most part things have gone very well. We love each other, spend a lot of time together, and feel very close. Lately, though, we've been having fights over silly issues. We're getting angry too often.

"We're noticing more and more differences in our

personalities and habits. He's a slob; I'm very neat. He stays up late; I go to bed early. I talk a lot; he often doesn't have much to say. He loves to watch sports on television; I prefer to watch what he calls 'chick flicks.' I do most of the household chores; unless I ask him to do a specific job, he just sits in his recliner.

"Our spats are happening more and more, and we can't seem to talk through and resolve our disagreements. We've been surprised at how angry we both have been. He'll raise his voice, and I'll cry. He'll walk away, and I'll follow him. He'll refuse to talk, and we'll hit another dead end. We want to stop fighting and get along like we used to."

In the New Marriage, there is plenty of love and passion. What's *missing* are the relational tools to successfully handle the male-female issues that are beginning to surface. The initial massive burst of infatuation runs out, and the ugly reality of living with the opposite sex rushes in.

The New Marriage pattern often occurs with individuals who have been married before. This type of new marriage is a real challenge because of baggage from previous marriages and the very real problems of stepparenting. Trying to build a marriage and blend two families at the same time is brutal, difficult work. Before you know it, the New Marriage can slip to Pretty Good, to Dead, and finally to "I Want a Divorce."

I tell couples in New Marriages that they have a

unique opportunity to avoid a lot of pain and heartache. By learning key interpersonal skills early in their marriage, they can keep their love robust and not develop the usual intimacy-killing behaviors.

The Great Marriage

A smiling couple walked up to me after one of my Marriage Seminars. The husband said, "Dave, thanks for the seminar. We learned a lot and will be applying your principles in our relationship. We've worked hard on our marriage over the years, and the work has paid off. We have a great marriage. We know how to adjust to our male-female differences, we communicate well, we identify and meet needs, we can resolve conflicts, we maintain a close spiritual bond, and our sex life is terrific.

"But you know what, Dave? We believe our marriage can get even better."

> It takes work to have a Great Marriage, but it's worth it.

The truth is, I don't talk to many couples like this. But there are couples out there in Great Marriages. My parents, Bill and Kathy Clarke, have a Great Marriage. The entire Clarke crew—my brother, Mark, and his family and my family—just celebrated my parents' fiftieth wedding anniversary in New York City. One evening in their hotel room, in front of all of us, my dad read a beautiful love tribute to my mom.

My parents are living proof that even a Great Marriage can get better over the years. They continue to seek to deepen their love and intimacy. It takes work, but it's worth it.

EVERY MARRIAGE CAN GET BETTER—A LOT BETTER

You and your spouse are in one of these marriage categories, aren't you? All five of these marriages have one thing in common: they need this book. You and your mate need this book.

I'm not saying this because I want it to be a runaway best seller so I can pay for my four kids' college educations and my three daughters' weddings. Okay, that's part of it. But the main reason is because every marriage needs work and can get better.

Here's the quality and intensity of love that God wants you to enjoy in your marriage:

> *"Put me like a seal over your heart,*
> *Like a seal on your arm.*
> *For love is as strong as death,*
> *Jealousy is as severe as Sheol;*
> *Its flashes are flashes of fire,*
> *The very flame of the Lord.*
> *Many waters cannot quench love,*
> *Nor will rivers overflow it;*
> *If a man were to give all the riches of his house for love,*
> *It would be utterly despised."*
>
> SONG OF SOLOMON 8:6–7

This kind of passionate, wonderful love is not just for a select few couples. Every married couple can experience it.

> *Marriage is the most difficult, complicated, and frustrating human relationship. It is also the one human relationship that can always get better and deeper and more intimate.*

YOUR MARRIAGE NEEDS A MAKEOVER

You picked up this book because you want a better marriage. Here's the good news: A better marriage is within your reach. Here's some even better news: God wants the same thing, and He'll help you perform the makeover. No matter what kind of marriage you're in now, it can become a loving and deeply intimate marriage.

Stop tolerating your mediocre—or worse—marriage. Stop making excuses. Stop stalling. Decide today to work hard and build a great marriage. Decide today to finish reading this book and apply the principles.

A PROVEN PLAN

When I was fresh out of my doctoral program in psychology and began counseling couples, I didn't know what I was doing. I knew a little bit about this and a little bit about that—communication, conflict resolution, male-female differences, family of origin issues, meeting needs—but I had no specific, focused, and effective plan to help couples change their marriages. I'd like to apologize to all the couples I saw in therapy the first few years of my practice. You, unfortunately, learned firsthand why they call it a *practice*.

But things have changed. Over the past twenty years,

God has guided me to develop a proven Marriage Makeover plan. I'm not into theories; I'm into what actually works for couples. I write only about what has succeeded in my clinical practice.

My Marriage Makeover plan works. It is biblically based, intensely practical, and clear and easy to understand. In each chapter, I include Snapshots, or letters, from spouses who have followed the makeover principles and specific steps for you and your mate to apply.

My plan has worked for hundreds of married couples with every possible set of marital problems. It will work for you. It will show you exactly how to make your marriage everything you want and need it to be—and everything that God wants it to be. Close. Intimate. Best friends. Passionate. Spiritually bonded. Needs met on a consistent basis. One flesh.

That's where we're going. If you're interested, come along for the ride. Oh, but you'll have to pedal. The Marriage Makeover does take some effort.

Your makeover begins with understanding the *obstacles* you and your mate will face in the process of changing your marriage.

SNAPSHOT
KATIE AND NEAL

Realization:
"We've lost that spark we used to have."—Katie

What went wrong?
- At best, the marriage is "okay."
- Couple time has diminished.
- "We're not as close as we used to be."

Current challenges:
- Temptation to settle for mediocrity.
- Rationalization that "it happens to everyone."

Next steps:
- Agree to pursue a "great" marriage.
- Start immediately.

MAKEOVER STEPS

1. In which of the five categories is your marriage? How long has your marriage been in this category?
2. Are you satisfied with your marriage as it is now? If not, why not?
3. Do you believe that, with God's help, your marriage can change?

Chapter 2
The Caveat

"HONEY, YOU'RE DRIVING ME CRAZY!"

The one problem with marriage is that a man and a woman have to live together. This is without question the worst idea anyone ever came up with. I mean, who are we kidding?

It's like putting a deer into the tiger's cage at the zoo and hoping the two of them can get along. I don't think so. There's going to be trouble. Bad trouble. And it won't take long.

> *The only thing more difficult than living with a member of the opposite sex is. . . Actually, there is nothing more difficult.*

I had a dream that a group of the world's greatest scientists, the most brilliant minds of our generation, came together at a retreat in the Swiss Alps (important retreats are always held in the Swiss Alps) to answer this important question: "What is the quickest and most effective way to drive a person insane?" The learned men and women went into a conference room and emerged five minutes later with a one-word answer: "Marriage."

We don't need a group of distinguished scientists to tell us what we already know, do we? If you're married, you know what I'm talking about. Is there anything more frustrating, nerve-wracking, and just plain exasperating than living with the opposite sex?

Dating is fantastic. Courtship is bliss. Engagement is super. The first few years of being husband and wife are usually great. But three to ten years into the marriage, some unpleasant revelations about your partner come to light. Dramatic gender differences, incredibly annoying habits, and grating personality weaknesses rise up and take a toll on your relationship.

Let me illustrate by describing the marriage I know best: mine.

THE CLARKE MARRIAGE

Sandy and I had been married for ten years. Our infatuation was long gone. Her weaknesses were painfully apparent. So were mine.

We had three small children—all girls. Or, rather, they had us. Mood shifts, tantrums, emotional scenes, sibling rivalry, hysterical laughter, insipid children's television shows with the worst acting ever filmed, and total chaos filled our home.

At least we weren't lonely. Sandy and I went three

solid years without going to the bathroom alone. We'd have an audience of one, two, or three fascinated spectators. The girls would make comments—some funny, some critical—about our "performances." It was like an Olympic event rated by three small and very opinionated judges. Fortunately, they didn't hold up score cards at the end of the bathroom exercises.

It was in the midst of these difficult circumstances that my beautiful blond wife began a campaign to drive me over the edge of sanity. Her ingenious diabolical plan was to use a bar of soap to make me go absolutely batty.

THE SLIVER OF SOAP

For the first ten years of our marriage, Sandy and I had no problems with our shared use of the bathroom shower. She showered in the evening, and I showered in the morning. Her shampoo was on the top shelf of the shower organizer; mine was on the middle shelf. She was in charge of buying her shampoo, and I bought my own.

Most important, we shared equally the replacing of the essential ingredient of every successful shower experience: the bar of soap. Sandy always kept a good supply of soap in the hall closet, a mere ten steps from our shower stall. It was an unspoken agreement that we took turns putting a fresh bar of soap in the shower whenever it was needed. The soap bar rested in the place of honor on the bottom shelf of the shower organizer.

As I'm sure you know, there's really nothing worse in a shower than a sliver of soap. When a bar of soap reaches a certain level of sliverness, it will not produce any lather, no matter how hard you rub it. Instead, it splits into two or more pieces, and when you try to rub the pieces in your hands, they fall to the shower floor. Once the fragments hit the floor, the centripetal force of the water hurries them toward the drain.

Of course, you quickly bend over and frantically try to collect the pieces before they slide out of reach and become irretrievably lodged in the drainpipe. You fail, and thus are forced to touch the slimy, hairy, incredibly nasty drain in order to clear it of the sliver pieces. Your hands are now infected with drain residue and eleven kinds of bacteria, but you can't wash them because *you don't have any soap!*

Sandy and I easily avoided this nightmare scenario with a highly effective procedure. Whenever the bar got down to a sliver, whoever happened to be showering at the time would walk to the hall closet and get a new bar. Of course, you only notice that the soap is a sliver *after* you're already in the shower and soaking wet. That's frustrating. Probably worth a minor level of exasperation.

Sandy and I operated for ten solid years on this guiding principle of shower etiquette: When faced with the dreaded sliver, follow seven simple steps out of respect for the shower component of the marriage.

1. Feel free to express the perfectly natural response of, "Oh, no! Not the sliver!"
2. Accept your fate with a wry grin and realize it's really no one's fault.
3. Turn off the water and get out of the shower.
4. Throw the sliver into the wastebasket, because soap slivers are useless and a health hazard.
5. Wrap a towel around yourself and walk the ten steps to the hall closet and get a new bar of soap.
6. Return to the shower with the new bar and resume your shower.
7. Feel good—maybe even a little proud—that you have done the right thing and kept your marriage running smoothly.

As I mentioned, this sliver of soap replacement system (SOSRS) worked beautifully for ten solid years. And then one day it screeched to a sudden and horrible stop. I will never forget the morning I stepped into the shower, got wet, and was faced with the dreaded sliver. I was shocked and appalled. I had taken a shower the previous morning and knew for a fact that I had used up the final suds of the bar. I had put the sliver back, knowing that Sandy would replace it with a fresh bar that evening. I had lucked out, and she would have to go through the seven steps of bar replacement.

But she hadn't replaced the bar! My whole showering world was turned upside down in an instant. Being a gracious and loving husband, I decided to give Sandy the benefit of the doubt. Maybe she was stressed. Caught up in the demands of caring for the three children. Yeah, that was it. I told myself this was just a one-time, out-of-the-ordinary occurrence.

So I replaced the bar and didn't say a word. I expected her to say something appreciative like, "Thanks for putting in that new bar of soap, Dave. I blew it, and I'm sorry. You are a kind and thoughtful husband. Will you forgive me?" Instead, she said nothing. I was slightly concerned about her lack of response, but I let it go.

Then it happened again. And again. And again. Sandy had stopped replacing the sliver! She never said a word. She just unilaterally decided that she was through replacing the sliver. It was unfair. It was selfish. It was just plain wrong. And even though I tried—really tried—to be the bigger person and take it in stride, her refusal to replace the sliver began to seriously bug me.

I mean, who did she think she was? The Queen of England? Was I her sliver replacement boy? How dare she leave me with the sliver every single time and act like nothing was wrong! She apparently didn't know who she was dealing with. I decided to fight back. Two could play at this game.

I decided to wait her out. As the new bar got smaller and smaller, I held the line. It got to be a sliver, and I knew she was expecting me to replace it. Dream on, baby! I was not going to do it. Not this boy. Not this time. The sliver got down to a nub. Down to two tiny pieces. Down to almost microscopic dimensions. And still Sandy did not replace it!

I held out for a week. I abandoned the extremely tiny sliver and used shampoo to wash. I used hand soap from the sink. I even used a new bar for a few days that I kept hidden in my underwear drawer. In utter desperation, I took the dramatic step of putting a new bar in its unopened package right beside the sliver. I had her now. All she had to do was throw out the sliver, open the new package, and take out the bar. But she wouldn't do it! What was the matter with her? Was she trying to send me to the mental hospital?

I finally confronted Sandy. It was mano a mano time. I walked up to her with the unbelievably small sliver of soap in my palm and asked, "What do you have to say for yourself?" Sandy, faking a confused look, replied, "What are you talking about?" Oh, she was good. Very good. I had to give her that.

I told her the whole story of the sliver replacement system and how she'd ruined it. She accused me of being crazy. Well, maybe I was, but she was the one who had driven me crazy! And then Sandy did what women often do when caught in a mistake. She went into a litany of all the jobs she did around the house. Her main point was that with all that she did for me and the kids, the very least I could do was replace the soap in the shower. Defeated, I had no response and had to skulk away.

I'm happy to report that we got past this unfortunate episode and can laugh about it now. It really wasn't a big deal. It was classic postinfatuation behavior, though, and it did push us farther apart at the time. By the way, guess who still replaces the sliver of soap every time? That's right. Me.

THE MANIAC ON THE ROAD

You've probably guessed by now that I also am capable of annoying habits. Even though I don't think it was in the same league as the sliver of soap, my driving used to cause Sandy significant distress.

About ten years into the marriage, Sandy began to comment on my driving. These were not nice, complimentary comments. She accused me of going too fast. Being in too much of a hurry. Taking too many chances. Being too hard on other drivers. Showing too much frustration. Being too aggressive. She actually called me "a maniac on the road."

I was insulted. I considered myself an excellent driver. I drove with confidence and complete safety. My driving skill was worthy of community awards, not petty criticism. I continued to drive my way, and Sandy continued her running commentary on what she saw as reckless and dangerous.

Okay, here's the story. When the kids were young, I had to drive a minivan. Fine. With kids in the car, I had to drive slowly. Again, fine. All the two-bit punks in their sleek sports cars could cut me off. Speed past me. Leave me choking in their exhaust fumes. Fine. I took my medicine. I paid my dues. But when the kids were a little older—Sandy and I had been married about ten or eleven years—I went back to my original, natural driving style.

Every time I got behind the wheel, I became Mr. Race Car Driver. It was a competition. A contest to see who could get down the road faster. It was me against all the other cars, except police cars, fire trucks, and ambulances.

I wanted to make every light. To me, a yellow light meant gun the accelerator and you can make it. I would seize every opening to get ahead of the pack. I lived to pass other cars and show them who was boss. People didn't expect a minivan to be weaving in and out of traffic, so that gave me an edge.

I used my horn constantly. I honked at slow drivers. Drivers who didn't get out of my way. Drivers who cost me a light. Drivers who were going too fast. Drivers who wouldn't turn left on the yellow. Drivers who wouldn't use their blinkers. Drivers who left their blinkers on. Drivers who drove ugly cars. Drivers with beautiful cars that I wanted.

Sandy hated all my horn use. She said it embarrassed her, and she was afraid it would provoke road rage in other motorists. I replied, "Honey, the horn is on the car to be used. I use it to clear the way ahead, to avoid accidents, to keep us safe, to teach others basic driving skills, and to express my feelings." She would shake her head and say to the girls, "Your father's going to kill us."

My proudest moments on the road were also the most annoying and frightening for Sandy. When some guy in a sports car or big pickup truck would cut me off, I'd take it as a personal insult. I'd blast him with my horn and then take off after him. I'd swerve in and out of traffic in an attempt to hunt him down like a dog. When I got back in front of him, I'd blast my horn in triumph and raise my fist in celebration. Like Snoopy did to the Red Baron. Sandy wasn't celebrating. She was fuming.

My driving was a source of bickering and tension for several years. It was one of a number of silly squabbles over insignificant issues that occurred about ten years into our marriage. My driving has improved. Sort of. The truth is, Sandy has adjusted and doesn't make it an issue very often. As I figured out with the sliver of soap, it's not a priority problem worth ongoing annoyance.

THE BATTLE OF THE PETTY

Marriage is filled with frustrated reactions to the growing list of your spouse's strange, nettlesome behaviors. How could you have married someone who turned out to be such a pest and a nuisance? Check out this brief catalog of personality and lifestyle differences. I think you'll recognize yourselves in some of these.

Thermostat Wars

One spouse is always hot. One is always cold. Complaining about the temperature and sneaking to the thermostat becomes commonplace.

Night Owl and Morning Glory

Morning Glory wakes up singing at 5:00 a.m. without an alarm but is brain-dead by 9:00 p.m. Night Owl comes alive at 9:00 p.m. and is ready to party but has to be hit with a cattle prod to get up in the morning.

Mr. Crude and Mrs. Manners

Mr. Crude belches and passes gas on a regular basis. He sees this as "being a man." It's also being a man not to feel too badly about it and to rarely say "Excuse me" after the offensive behavior. Mrs. Manners is horrified and offended by his complete lack of taste.

> *In Europe, belching after a meal is an expected and cherished behavior. Wives are thrilled by it. The moral: Marry a European woman or move to Europe if you want to keep barking out those belches.*

Pack Rat and Garage Saler

The Pack Rat keeps everything, including every school paper the children bring home. The Pack Rat hogs every square inch of storage room to hoard the treasure trove of trivialities and minutia. The Garage Saler wants to sell everything and feels buried alive in a mountain of useless stuff.

The Slob and the Neatnik

One spouse is a rumpled, crumpled, and disorganized mess maker who never puts anything away and sees no reason to clean when the place is just going to get dirty again. The Neatnik wants to live in a museum of order and cleanliness and sees messiness as evidence of a weak, disturbed mind.

Ratty Clothes Man

This husband parades around in twenty-year-old, thread-bare T-shirts, college sweatshirts, and gym shorts from his high school days. His old clothes are filled with holes and hideous stains, but he considers them old friends. He's horribly out of fashion, but he's comfortable.

The Closet Hog

The wife fills her closet, his closet, and parts of other closets with her amazing quantity and variety of clothes and her incredible assortment of shoes, purses, belts, hats, and pieces of jewelry. She continues to buy more closet-hogging items, even though there's no room left and she can't possibly wear all the things she already has. On the bright side, she keeps the economy going.

The Incredible Phone-Talking Woman

She talks on the telephone just about every free waking

minute. She has an impressive array of family and friends, and she must keep in daily contact with all of them. No topic of conversation is unimportant. The husband hears the same stories repeated over and over as he struggles to keep his brain from exploding.

Never on Time

One spouse is chronically late for everything. Church. Social events. School activities. Doctor appointments. Work. Airline flights. He or she is usually married to someone who wants to be fifteen minutes early for everything. They make a tough combination.

I'm Going to Die—Again

This partner thinks that every illness or pain is a symptom of a final, fatal disease. Pain in the chest means catastrophic heart problems. Pain in the back means the kidneys are failing. Pain in the rear (he or she has become a pain in the rear to the spouse) means rectal cancer. And so on.

I could go on and on. There are sunny optimists married to gloom-and-doom pessimists. Bedroom television watchers who have to have the set on to go to sleep. Physical fitness enthusiasts who pressure the spouse to work out and consume fruit drinks. Vegetarians. Lip-smacking, slurping soup eaters. Snorers. Bed hogs. Toss and turners. Putterers. And you could probably add a few of your own.

IT'S GOING TO GET WORSE BEFORE IT GETS BETTER

Every married couple must put up with at least a few annoying habits and differences, and some can even be amusing. The ability to laugh at ourselves helps to lessen the tension. What's *not* funny is that some of these differences push us farther apart. As our differences become more and more obvious, our marriages take more hits more often, even if we're not yet entirely aware of it.

Just about every married couple experiences a breakdown in intimacy, where fewer and fewer needs are met in the relationship, and our emotional, spiritual, and physical connections are diminished. It doesn't happen right away, but it happens. It's a natural and inevitable result of living with a member of the opposite sex.

But there is hope. Following my Marriage Makeover plan will reverse the decline of intimacy and get your relationship back on track. That's what it's designed to do and that's what it will do.

SNAPSHOT
BRUCE AND CINDY

Realization:
"We didn't get married to drive each other nuts and bicker over silly issues."
—Bruce

What went wrong?
- Cindy's energy and busyness leave Bruce feeling overlooked.
- Bruce's messiness annoys the tidy Cindy.
- "Some of your habits are really starting to bug me."

Current challenges:
- Cindy: Find time to relax and work on marriage.
- Bruce: Put differences behind and focus on the positive.

Next steps:
- Strive for "crazy *about* you," not "crazy *because* of you."
- Commit to consciously avoiding those habits that annoy each other.

1. Talk about your spouse's annoying habits that drive you crazy. Be specific. Don't be mean; just be honest. Try to have a lighthearted, humorous attitude about these habits.
2. Which Battle of the Petty scenarios have been true in your marriage?
3. Are you still significantly upset and bothered by your partner's annoying habit or habits? If so, commit out loud that you will work to release your irritation as you follow the Makeover Steps described in the next several chapters. Also, make this same commitment in prayer with your spouse.

Chapter 3
The Myth of the Marriage

INFATUATION CAN LAST FOREVER

Let me take you back in time to the early days of your relationship. Can you picture those days? You meet, and you both know there's a spark of mutual interest and desire. You're clicking as you've never clicked with anyone before. The spark is leaping into a flame of supercharged emotions, and you're falling in love.

Excitement that sets your hearts racing. Passion off the charts. A wonderful feeling of closeness. Music in the air. Candlelight dinners. Long talks. Laughter. The two of you are riding the crest of a massive wave of feel-good vibes and intense love.

Falling in love is hormonal. It's a biochemical reaction. It's just like what happens at the zoo during mating season. The animals stir in their cages and are driven to mate and procreate by instinctive forces they don't understand. The male orangutan sidles over on his knuckles to a female and says in ape talk, "Hey, baby, new here at the zoo? You're looking good today." She replies, "I've been here in this same cage with you for ten years, Sparky. But I have to tell you, big boy, I like what I see. Come and get me."

You two orangutans—I mean, humans—are ecstatic. Exhilarated. Intoxicated with happiness. Everything is perfect. Your partner is perfect. Your relationship is perfect. You feel all your needs are met in this person. Totally and completely. You have no complaints at all. You have found your soul mate. You marvel at how well you get along and how much you have in common. You agree on everything. You have no conflicts. You have no problems of any kind. Nothing can go wrong.

Your partner can slam the car door on your hand, and it's okay. It's all good. "It's fine, sweetheart. Really. Now whenever I look at my crippled hand, I'll think of you."

Your physical relationship is out of this world. Your touch is charged with electricity. You have trouble keeping your hands off of each other. Each kiss is unbelievable. Long, wet, and delicious. Even potato chip breath smells good. When your lips meet, fireworks go off, birds sing, and world peace is a little closer.

You think your communication as a couple is terrific. You can talk for hours and not get tired of each other. You believe you're reaching deep levels of emotional connection and understanding. Everything your partner says seems profound and personal and revealing:

"I like that dress."
"I had a lousy day at work."
"I think there's a rock in my shoe."
"Bugs Bunny is my favorite cartoon character."

These statements are fascinating, stimulating, and devastatingly insightful to you. Actually, they aren't, but in the fiery glow of infatuation, they seem to be.

WHEN INFATUATION IS OVER, IT'S OVER

There's a term for these incredibly happy, cloud-nine days. It's *infatuation*. Oh, what a marvelous stage in a relationship! And it's a God-designed stage. He wants you to have it. It's part of His plan for bringing two people together and getting them married. God knows that without infatuation, no one would ever get married.

Notice I used the word *stage*. That's because infatuation is designed to be only temporary. After one to three years, it ends. With a thud! Never to return. Infatuation gets you to the wedding, but it's not going to carry you for fifty or sixty years of marital bliss. Within the first few years of most marriages, the infatuation stage ends. And when it's over, it's over.

In infatuation's place comes real life—two unbelievably different individuals trying to live together without killing each other or driving each other crazy. You notice flaws in your once-perfect partner. Quite a few, actually. You're still perfect, of course, but your spouse definitely isn't. You don't see eye to eye on everything. You disagree. You're right, and your spouse is wrong. The bloom is clearly off the rose, and things start to get messy and difficult. Welcome to marriage.

BEFORE AND AFTER THE MARRIAGE

Just a few years (and sometimes only a few months) into your marriage, your view of your partner changes. Infatuation has evaporated, and you can now see all of his or her frustrating, disgusting, and terribly disappointing weaknesses. Suddenly, the knot you tied looks more like a ball and chain.

I'll illustrate this before-and-after-marriage change by using a newly married couple: Marv and Marge.

Before Marriage: "Marge is kind of disorganized. It's cute. She has trouble finding her keys."

After Marriage: "The woman is a slob! You would not believe the filth and clutter she creates. How can a grown woman live that way? Every square inch of the top of our tables, bureaus, and kitchen counters is filled with stacks of her stuff. And, so help me, I don't know what I'm going to do if I have to keep waiting while she roots through her mountain of debris looking for those stupid keys!"

Before Marriage: "Marv is very affectionate. He likes to touch me. I know it's an expression of his love. It feels great to be wanted. He makes me feel beautiful and desirable."

After Marriage: "All he thinks about is sex! He's an animal! Does he have some kind of glandular problem? Every day is like mating season. He's always pawing at me!"

Before Marriage: "Marge can't cook. It's funny how she

can't even boil water. I'm not marrying her for her cooking ability."

After Marriage: "If I'm not starving to death, I'm struggling not to spit up what she's cooked. The health department would shut down her kitchen if they knew what was going on in there. Is she trying to poison me?"

Before Marriage: "Marv is so helpful and does so many things for me. He goes grocery shopping with me, goes to the mall with me, runs errands for me, washes my car, and is always asking what he can do to make my life easier."

After Marriage: "You have never seen a lazier man in your life! I'm surprised he can hold a job. He has energy only for sex. He'd rather face a firing squad than go the mall. He sits on the couch clicking that stupid remote or plays those silly computer games. It takes a court order or the business end of a shotgun to get him to do a household chore. He tells me he pulls his weight around the house. I tell him he *puts* his weight—on the couch."

Before Marriage: "Marge is bubbly and is *so* expressive. She's never at a loss for words. I love her stories. There's never a lull in our conversations."

After Marriage: "I pray every day for one lull in a conversation. Just one! The woman never stops talking! She doesn't even take a breath. She beats her gums all day long, and I can't take it much longer. Every thought and feeling she has is spoken. Please! Make her stop!"

Before Marriage: "Marv is the strong, silent type. He doesn't talk that much, but that's okay. He's a good listener. I feel safe and secure with him. We can just be together without talking, and it's beautiful."

After Marriage: "He talks to the dog more than he talks to me! The man is a stick! The only sound he makes is when he clears his throat. What he's thinking and feeling is the world's greatest mystery. I am seriously considering getting him checked for brain damage."

These scenarios sound familiar? I'll bet they do. Before marriage we're in Fantasyland. After marriage we enter Realityland. We slowly realize with horror who we've really married.

Every married couple goes through this rude transition from infatuation to the reality of married life. No one warns us that this is going to happen! Even if someone did, we wouldn't listen. We're convinced that we'll be the exception. Unfortunately, there are no exceptions.

Now, it's bad enough at this point with just the two of you living together. But it's about to get worse. Much worse. When you add another human being to the equation, the breakdown of your perfect love life accelerates.

GAIN A CHILD, LOSE EVERYTHING ELSE

Your beautiful bouncing baby has arrived. Your new child is an exciting addition to the family and a precious gift from God. But it dawns on you fairly quickly that when you have a child, you lose many things.

You lose your *money*. The thousands of dollars it costs just to bring a baby into the world is only the beginning of the emptying of your bank account. Clothes, blankets, crib, bumper pads, onesies, booties, tiny caps, baby shampoo, baby soap, lotion for the frequent diaper rashes, changing table, diapers by the hundreds, diaper bag, stroller, car seat, walker, pacifiers, spit-up rags, one thousand toys, mobiles, a lifetime supply of cereal and crackers, formula, a baby book, a college fund, and on and on and on the list goes.

You lose your *sleep*. Babies scream unpredictably throughout the day and night. Babies scream when hungry. When thirsty. When their diapers are loaded. When Mommy leaves the room. When the slightest bit of discomfort occurs. When the blanket shifts. When the all important pacifier is spit out and gets wedged between the crib and the wall where a team of CSIs couldn't find it. When the room is dark. When their tummies are upset. When they want company and a warm chest to snuggle against. When happy. When sad. When frustrated. When you've just dropped off to sleep after the last episode of screaming.

You lose your *personal time* and your *couple time*. That screaming, pooping, belching, and spitting-up little bundle of neediness is always around! Even when you're together, the baby is there and in the spotlight.

You lose your *sex*. It's just about impossible to have

regular sex when you're exhausted, irritable, and spending every waking minute taking care of a baby. How ironic that your baby is both the product of your sex life and the reason for its demise.

You lose your *ability to be a rational, caring, unselfish person*. Especially at night. When the lights go out and the baby is in the crib, it's survival time. It's every parent for himself or herself. You become sleep commandos who will do anything—and I mean anything—for a few extra winks. The baby cries, and you lie perfectly still, pretending to be asleep. You feel no guilt, only a dogged determination to outlast your spouse. In this high-stakes game of cat and mouse, whoever moves first loses and has to deal with the screaming tyrant. Sure, your spouse will hate your guts, but it's only temporary, and it's a price you're willing to pay to take care of yourself.

You lose your *sports car*. This one really hurts the men. Like anyone else cares. Driving a minivan that your wife picked out strips you of your manhood. You become an automotive eunuch. As people on foot and kids on bikes go faster than your minivan, you endure the looks of pity from men in Corvettes, BMWs, and Porsches.

But what you really lose is your *marriage*. When the baby arrives, your marriage goes. At least temporarily. Your relationship is suspended because the child becomes the center of your lives. It happens to every couple. The second your first child is born, you go from being marriage-centered to child-centered.

The wife becomes a mom and is obsessed with nurturing and caring for her baby. *You* were once her baby! Her attention shifts from husband to child. It has to! She's not wrong in doing this. It's natural and God-directed. Unfortunately, husbands often feel left out, neglected, and not a priority. The marriage suffers.

By the way, if you have another child, the losses and disruption to your marriage are doubled, at least at first. A third child? Triple it. Believe me, I know what I'm talking about. Sandy and I have four children. You do the math.

NOW, FOR THE TRUTH

The truth is, infatuation doesn't last. It's wonderful, but it's only a phase. It *never* lasts. It *can't* last. At least not the way it is at the beginning of a marriage. Making a marriage successful and intimate is hard work, and you must keep up the hard work to maintain your love. But here's a promise: After your Marriage Makeover, those same wonderful feelings of infatuation—but deeper now and based on experience—will return, and will last a lifetime.

The truth is that children bring tremendous challenges to a marriage. Kids are wonderful, and they're gifts from God, but the relentless pressure they apply forces a husband and wife to make adjustments they don't know how to make.

The truth is that our American culture is clueless about what it takes to make a marriage work. But God isn't. God created marriage, and He knows exactly what it takes to make it work. Not just work—*thrive*.

What do you do when your infatuation has run out, your differences and habits are driving you crazy, and your children have taken over your lives? You do a Marriage Makeover. A makeover based on God's Word, the Bible.

You've waited long enough for a great marriage. Let's get started on your makeover.

Realization:
"It's time for us to love each other the way God says to love."—Carolyn

What went wrong?
- Bought into the myth of perpetual infatuation.
- Blending two families was "brutally hard."

Current challenges:
- "The kids have come between us."
- Individual approach to problems has marriage on brink of divorce.

Next steps:
- Acknowledge primary interest in repairing marriage.
- Agree to pursue changes in God's biblical way.

1. Talk with your spouse about your infatuation stage. Recall how God brought you together. Describe the feelings you had and some specific memories from that wonderful stage.

2. When did your infatuation end? Which of the before-and-after marriage scenarios sounds most familiar? Discuss the weaknesses you began to see in your spouse.

3. If you have children, talk about how they have affected your marriage. Be honest and specific about how having a child—or more than one—has negatively affected your marriage relationship.

4. What cultural myths about marriage have you believed? What has been the effect of believing these myths?

Chapter 4
Marriage Makeover Achievement 1

YOUR IMPOSSIBLE MISSION TEAM

Remember *Mission Impossible*, the great television show that ran from 1966 to 1973? Peter Graves played Jim Phelps, the unflappable leader of the Impossible Mission Force, an elite, highly trained, and supersecret team of American government agents. Jim and his small, hand-picked team of specialists were given assignments that were unbelievably difficult, extremely dangerous, and, well—impossible.

At the beginning of every show, Jim would be given his assignment by a guy with a deep voice speaking on an audiocassette tape. After Jim had listened to the hair-raising, spine-tingling description of the mission, the tape would self-destruct in a puff of smoke. Each time, Jim was assured that if he or any of his team were caught or killed in carrying out the mission, those who sent them would "disavow any knowledge" of their activities.

Just one time, I wanted Jim to say, "Accept this mission? What? Are you, crazy? Forget it! I don't want to die. Get some other sucker to do it." Of course, Jim never did that. He was too cool and gutsy. He always said yes, gathered his IMF team, and went to work.

How were Jim Phelps and his group of associates able to pull off these impossible missions? Two reasons:

1. *Mission Impossible* was a television show, and the successful outcomes were written into the script. The show would have been over if the bad guys had won.
2. Jim Phelps and his agents worked as a *team*. They achieved their goals only by relying on each other. Supporting each other. Working together. Alone, they were helpless and didn't stand a chance. Together, they were strong and effective. No task was impossible.

You have an impossible mission. To do a Marriage Makeover. It can be done, but not alone. Just like Jim Phelps, you *must create a support team*.

YOUR OPPOSITION IS FIERCE

Alone, you have zero chance to complete a successful Marriage Makeover. If you're operating without a team, the opposition you'll face will blow you out of the water. What is your opposition? It will strike at three levels.

The first level of opposition is *you*. That's right, *you*. Your own resistance to change will be a major obstacle. You want to change. You know you need to be different.

You want a better marriage. It's one of the desires of your heart. But still you fight the necessary changes. That's human nature. We psychologists call it *homeostasis*: the tendency to remain the same.

Change is tough. Change is painful. Change requires hard work. Change forces you to look in the mirror and admit your flaws. Change demands vulnerability and risk. You simply must have a team to motivate you and push you along the path of change. Your team will deliver the multiple kicks in the pants you need to keep going.

The second level of opposition is *habit*. Your old marital patterns will die hard. It has taken years to develop the various unhealthy components of your relationship, and they won't go away easily or quietly. Your dysfunctional, intimacy-robbing interactions are entrenched. Automatic. Set in concrete. Your team members will provide the encouragement and support needed for you to break out of these old, damaging patterns.

The third level of opposition is *spiritual warfare*. First Peter 5:8 paints a vivid, chilling picture of the enemy you're up against: "Be of sober spirit, be on the alert. Your adversary, the devil, prowls about like a roaring lion, seeking someone to devour."

Guess who Satan wants to devour? You. Your mate. And your marriage. Satan does not want you to have a Marriage Makeover. That's putting it mildly. He hates you, and he hates your marriage. He wants to destroy your relationship.

The Bible, from Genesis through Revelation, describes Israel's relationship with God and our relationship with Jesus Christ in terms of a marriage (Hosea 2:19–20; Ephesians 5:31–32). So, when Satan attacks a Christian's marriage, he is also attacking the Christian's relationship with God. Christian marriages are a prime target for Satan, because he knows if he can ruin them, the horrible fallout will touch many lives for years to come. He also knows that if Christian marriages fail, people will think that Christianity doesn't work.

If Satan fails in his ceaseless efforts to devastate your marriage, he'll still do what he can to make you miserable in your marriage. He'll even settle for keeping you stuck in a mediocre marriage.

Don't face this most dangerous foe alone. He'll win every time. He's too good. He's too clever. Too strong. To beat him and the demons he's assigned to your marriage, you must take the team approach. Empowered by the Lord, you and your team can square off against Satan and win.

THE BIBLE SAYS "TEAM UP"
God doesn't want us to live our lives on our own. He wants every Christian to be on a team:

> *Bear one another's burdens, and thus fulfill the law of Christ.*
> GALATIANS 6:2

> *Two are better than one because they have a good return for their labor. For if either of them falls, the one will lift up his*

companion. But woe to the one who falls when there is not another to lift him up. Furthermore, if two lie down together they keep warm, but how can one be warm alone? And if one can overpower him who is alone, two can resist him. A cord of three strands is not quickly torn apart.

ECCLESIASTES 4:9–12

"Again I say to you, that if two of you agree on earth about anything that they may ask, it shall be done for them by My Father who is in heaven. For where two or three have gathered together in My name, there I am in their midst."

MATTHEW 18:19–20

That's pretty clear, isn't it? God wants no one to ride alone on the Christian journey. No one.

The apostle Paul, that amazing Christian dynamo whose faith in Christ energized the early church and spearheaded the spread of Christianity, always operated as part of a team. Paul developed discipling/mentoring relationships with many New Testament followers of Christ, including Timothy, Titus, Barnabas, John Mark, Silas, Aquila and Priscilla, and Peter, to name a few.

Like Paul, you need a team. Let me introduce you to your team.

You and Your Spouse

Who comes to mind when you think of great teams? Because I love humor, I think of comedy teams such as Laurel and Hardy, Abbott and Costello, Martin and Lewis, Hope and Crosby, Desi and Lucy, Burns and

Allen, Stiller and Meara.

As we have seen in the first two chapters, some of your relationship dynamics as a couple may make you look like a comedy team. Marriage can be very funny, but God is also very serious about wanting your marriage to succeed. When He thinks of great teams, He thinks of your marriage. No, really! He does! He thinks of your marriage, and my marriage, and every other marriage between Christians. How can I say this? Here's how: "For this reason a man shall leave his father and his mother, and be joined to his wife; and they shall become one flesh" (Genesis 2:24, emphasis added).

Those two words, "one flesh," are God's way of saying that He wants you and your spouse to be one of the world's greatest—and closest—teams. "One flesh" means complete and total unity. You are no longer two persons. You are one. One spiritually, emotionally, and physically. As you move through the makeover process, your spouse will be the most important human member of your support team. As you approach the Makeover Achievement Steps, I urge you to act like one flesh, *even if you don't feel like it*. Read each chapter and discuss the steps together. By *together*, I mean sitting side by side, reading the same material at the same time. The faster reader simply places his or her finger at the bottom of the page when finished and waits for the other team member to catch up. Discuss and apply the makeover steps *together*. Ask your spouse lots of questions about how he or she feels about the points you have read.

If your spouse refuses to join you in this project, don't be discouraged. Don't let your disappointment stop you from reading on your own. You will not be alone. Lean on the other members of your support team as you read and carry out the Makeover Steps that apply to you. You will become a different and better spouse, and your new behavior may entice your partner to change.

You and Your Accountability Partner

Both spouses must also find a person who will serve as an accountability partner. Your part of the Marriage Makeover will be difficult. Very difficult. To become the husband or wife that God wants you to be, you will need a same-sex confidant to walk beside you every step of the way.

Here's your accountability partner's job description:

> Loves Jesus.
> Loves you.
> Is not a family member.
> Can keep secrets.
> Will confront.
> Will comfort.
> Will encourage.
> Will listen.
> Will make time on a regular basis to talk and pray with you.

This person may be your age or may be older or younger. This person may already be a friend or someone you haven't met. Preferably, he or she will be married—and, from everything you know, *happily* married. Your partner's marriage may not be perfect, of course, but it should be strong and stable and healthy. Your relationship may be one-way, with your friend serving as a mentor to you, or it may be a mutual relationship, with the two of you holding each other accountable for the Makeover Steps.

I recommend a once-a-week, face-to-face meeting with your accountability partner. The meeting should be in a quiet and private setting and should last at least an hour. It takes time to learn the Makeover Steps well. You will discuss the specific Makeover Achievements you are working on and the obstacles you are encountering in the change process. End each meeting with prayer.

Use phone contact as needed to keep your communication current. Sometimes you will need to vent or ask for a shot of encouragement during the week. That's what phones and accountability partners are for. Make these calls, and don't feel guilty about doing so.

Start thinking right now about who can be your accountability partner. Make a list of candidates. Pray that God will direct you to the right person. If you can't think of anyone, go to your pastor and ask him to help you find someone. Sometimes it can be very difficult to find this person, for a variety of reasons. But God will help you if you don't give up. When you have identified one or more possibilities, summon your courage, and go ask these individuals to serve in this accountability role. The right person will be willing and will see it as a kindness to a brother or sister and as a way to serve the Lord.

You and Your Mentor Couple
In my opinion, one of the greatest ideas in a church-based marriage ministry is the mentor couple. Can you imagine having a married couple—solid, mature, loving, happy, experienced, and God-centered—coming alongside you and your mate to help you face your problems and improve your marriage? Can you imagine talking with a couple who has been where you are now? A couple who has struggled with the same tough issues and found answers that worked?

Can you imagine how helpful a relationship like this would be? I think you can. A mentor couple is an absolute gold mine. I can't overstate the power and positive, relationship-changing influence a mentor couple can bring to your Marriage Makeover journey.

Pray with your spouse that God will lead you to a mentor couple. This couple is almost certainly in your church. Look for couples who—as best you can determine—have built great, godly marriages over a period of several years and have a reputation confirming this. Make a list. Ask your pastor for names. With the husband leading, go and ask your top choice.

Tell your mentor couple that you and your spouse are

working through this book, and you'd like help in applying the makeover principles. Ask them if they would meet you and your spouse once every two weeks for an hour. At these meetings, you will discuss the specific Makeover Achievements you are addressing. You need to be held accountable. You need encouragement. You need their experience in overcoming obstacles. You need prayer.

If your spouse will not meet with the mentor couple, go on your own. With their help and guidance, you will make significant changes.

You and Your Local Church

God wants you and your spouse in church on a regular basis. He has chosen the local church as His vehicle to change the world. God says do not get out of the habit of attending church (Hebrews 10:25), but be committed and active members (Acts 2:42; Ephesians 4:14–16).

You need a local church that will support you emotionally and spiritually as you work to change your marriage. You need a church where you can find accountability partners and a mentor couple. You need a church where the Bible is taught from the pulpit. You need a church where you can be in a Sunday Bible class, a women's or men's Bible study and fellowship group, a support group, or a life group where you will receive the encouragement and emotional connections that smaller groups like these can provide. You need a church where you can worship God and serve Him with your gifts.

Though not essential, it is preferable to be in a church with a strong men's ministry, women's ministry, and marriage ministry. A church with these programs can meet your relational needs, expose you to good Christian role models, and provide biblical teaching on how to build a great marriage.

You and God

The most important member of your support team is God. He is the One who created you and your spouse. He is the One who brought you together. He is the One who will change your marriage. He is the One who will provide the power you need to follow through on the Marriage Makeover Steps. Everyone on your team will make significant contributions, but it will be God who gets the job done.

I urge each of you to work diligently on your personal relationship with God as you move through the Marriage Makeover. It's easy to drift from God when your marriage is struggling, but you can't afford to let that happen. You must move closer to your heavenly Father, because He is the only One who can sustain you and give you the marriage you want so much and need.

Spend time with God every day. Just you and God in a quiet place. This could be early in the morning, before you go to bed, or on your lunch break. Talk with Him. Thank Him for all He has done for you. Praise and adore Him for who He is. Tell Him the honest truth about your personal and marital pain. Make specific requests. Ask Him for help in applying this book's steps, and ask Him to help your spouse apply the steps.

Read the Bible and meditate on it. Be quiet and listen to what God is saying to you through His Word and the Holy Spirit. The closer you are to God, the closer you will be to a brand-new marriage.

Realization:
"I've always been a lone ranger—I thought that made me a man."—Dan

What went wrong?
- Dan believed he could solve all his marriage problems on his own.
- Dan has been stubborn, proud, and unwilling to ask for help.

What's going right?
- Dan asked for help and found support, wisdom, and encouragement.
- Accountability partner and mentor couple have contributed to marriage improvement.
- Church attendance, men's fellowship, and quiet time have provided a spiritual boost.

Next steps:
- Maintain connection with the "team."
- Continue performing the Makeover Steps with Betty.

1. Discuss with your spouse the opposition to your Marriage Makeover. What will get in the way of changing your marriage? What—both generally and specifically—will Satan do to stop you? What has happened in the past to hurt your marriage and sabotage your efforts to improve your relationship? You both know these so well. What part of the relationship will be the most difficult for you to change?

2. Ask your spouse to work on the Makeover Steps with you. Agree that you will be a team and will go through the chapters together.

3. Tell your spouse whom you have written on your list of possible accountability partners. Commit to finding and enlisting this person in the next two weeks.

4. With your spouse, develop a list of potential mentor couples. Commit to finding and enlisting this couple in the next two weeks.

5. If you don't have a local church, find one as soon as you can. If you attend one now, stay faithful in attendance and get involved in at least one area of ministry or service.

6. Commit to your spouse that you will spend personal time daily with God: praying, listening, and reading the Bible and other helpful materials.

Chapter 5
Marriage Makeover Achievement 2

IT'S ABOUT TIME!

Near the end of every married couple's first therapy session with me, I ask the same question: "How much face-to-face, no-distractions-allowed, just-the-two-of-you-together time do you spend in the average week?" Ninety-nine percent give the same answer: "Not much, if any."

One of my first jobs as a therapist is to convince these couples to establish a regular, daily, twenty- to thirty-minute communication time. I tell them that this planned, intentional block of time will be a crucial, wholly indispensable ingredient in the makeover of their marriage.

WHY TIME TOGETHER IS SO IMPORTANT

Most of these couples ask why time together is so important. Here's what I tell them: Part of the breakdown of your marriage is the gradual loss of time together. In the infatuation stage, you can't get enough of each other. You spend hours together each week talking, laughing, walking hand in hand, kissing, and making out. But after infatuation, your marriage begins to break down, and the amount of time you spend together goes down and down and down. You become masters at avoiding each other. You lose your ability to communicate, and you stop trying to connect emotionally. Pretty soon your one-on-one time together is practically nonexistent.

Without time together, you have no marriage, and you have no way to rebuild the relationship. Without time together, you can't communicate (except to say, "Be sure to pick up Johnny this afternoon," or "The garbage has to be put out today"). If you can't communicate, you can't create intimacy *of any kind*. You can't be emotionally intimate. You can't be spiritually intimate. You may have sex, but you can't be truly intimate.

> *Time together is a critical prerequisite to intimacy.*
> *Time does not guarantee intimacy, but it is simply*
> *necessary for intimacy to be created.*

Without time together, you'll end up as roommates. Parents. Business associates. But not lovers. Definitely not lovers.

Without time together, you can't work on and improve any area of your relationship. You're stuck, and you'll stay stuck. Actually, you won't stay stuck. Your marriage will get worse and worse, less and less fulfilling, the longer you are without time together.

With one-on-one time together, you can rebuild your

marriage. With time together, you can successfully complete your Marriage Makeover. You can figure out what happened to cause your problems. You can begin identifying and meeting your real needs. Your time together will generate true, God-designed intimacy and become the centerpiece of your new marriage.

MAKING COUPLE TIME IS TOUGH

After my brilliant and impassioned explanation of the essential nature of time together, couples jump to their feet in my office and enthusiastically cry out: "Yes! We get it! You're right! How could we have been so blind? Time together! Of course! We will do it. Just tell us how."

Actually, this response is not what typically happens. In fact, it's not even close. Couples know I'm right, but they don't like it. They squirm uncomfortably and start to sweat. The thought of spending a half-hour alone with each other every day scares them. Most of them haven't talked—really talked—for years. They're completely out of practice.

Why wouldn't it be easy to make daily time for each other? It's common sense that every relationship requires time to fix problems. Time to grow. Time to get closer. The same is true of our relationship with God. It's not easy for these couples because their marital breakdown has pushed them apart and robbed them of their ability to communicate. They can't remember the last time they had a good, deep, enjoyable, stimulating, and intimate conversation. They've forgotten how to do it. They're no longer the close friends who loved to talk. The prospect of facing one another in a private, quiet place in their home feels awkward. Painful. Threatening.

Couples fight tooth and nail against my recommendation of regular couple times. Most of the excuses I've heard over the years fall into seven categories. Here they are, along with my responses:

"HERE'S WHY WE CAN'T DO COUPLE TIME"

Couple: "You don't understand, Dave. We're too busy."
Me: "Baloney. You always make time for what's important to you. If you needed chemotherapy treatments to live, I'll bet you wouldn't miss one appointment. If you want to keep your *marriage* alive, you need time together."

Couple: "Our kids get in the way. By the time they get to bed, it's too late for us to have any time together."
Me: "What do you mean, 'By the time they get to bed'? It's your job to put them to bed early enough, according to their age, so that you can build your marriage. Stop being bedtime wimps and take charge. If you have small kids, follow the strategy that Sandy and I used for years. We put the kids in their rooms no later than 8:00 p.m. and locked their doors. That's right. We reversed the locks and imprisoned them to keep them from coming out and bugging us. We left the night-light on. I said to each child: 'Your day is now over. Our day is just beginning.'

We then went immediately to the living room couch for our thirty-minute couple time. A few hours later, when we went to bed, we opened their doors for the night. We often found their sleeping bodies wedged against the doors, little hands stretched out toward the hall light. Pitiful. We scooped them up and put them in their beds. No, they weren't traumatized. They got the sleep they needed, and we got the time we needed to grow intimacy in our marriage.

"If you have teenagers, first let me say, 'I'm sorry. My heart goes out to you. I feel your pain.' Simply tell your teens to stay in their rooms for the next thirty minutes while you have your private couple time. They'll already be in their rooms because they hate you. If, for some crazy reason, your teens don't want to go to their rooms, start kissing and making out in front of them. They'll gag and run screaming to their rooms. They might even leave the country."

Couple: "We talk enough during the day. We're communicating. We don't need a specific daily time to talk." **Me:** "No, you're not talking enough during the day. That's just superficial chatter. You're not reaching any real depth. Discussing the weather, who's going to pick up the dry cleaning, and what's for dinner doesn't create intimacy. You need focused, intentional in-person couple time to generate real closeness."

Couple: "We watch television almost every night. We'd hate to miss our favorite shows."

Me: "You're kidding, right? The television is more important than your marriage? You would rather watch other people communicate than do it yourselves? What do you think the VCR is for? Tape your shows and watch them after your couple time. Once you get into the flow, your couple times will be much more entertaining than the drivel on television."

Couple: "We need personal alone time each day. You know, to get some space. To unwind and de-stress."

Me: "That's fine—if you're single. But you're married, and your marriage is more important than your need for space. Have your daily couple time first. It's actually a great way to unwind and clean the stress out of your systems. Connecting with your beloved will invigorate and energize you. After your couple time, you can each get some alone time."

Couple: "We don't want to schedule times to talk. That seems too rigid and forced. We want our communication to be spontaneous, to just happen."

Me: "Good, deep communication doesn't just happen. The two of you have to make it happen. When was your last great spontaneous conversation? Yeah, I thought so. Intimacy is spontaneous and unpredictable, but you have to give yourselves opportunities to experience it. The more couple times you schedule each week, the more opportunities for intimacy you will have."

Couple: "We don't make couple time because we have no idea what to talk about. I guess we're out of sync and don't know what to say to each other. We lost that wonderful skill we had."

Me: "I buy that. I believe you. I can help you with conversational material. I'm going to tell you exactly what to talk about."

WHAT COUPLE TIME LOOKS LIKE

Sit down over the weekend and schedule your couple times for the upcoming week. Nail down specific days and times, taking into consideration any activities that might prevent these times. Put them on your calendar, in your day-timers, and in your PDA. Don't wing it and hope to pull off these meetings without any planning. They'll never happen. Schedule them.

Make it your goal to meet every day. Life will probably prevent you from meeting seven days a week, but by aiming high, you will be able to squeeze in the highest possible number of couple times. I tell my clients, "Shoot for seven and get four." A minimum of four couple times a week will be enough to generate connection and closeness.

Pick the times that are best for both of you (not always an easy task). It doesn't matter when you meet as long as you sit down together for twenty to thirty minutes during the day. It could be in the morning, at lunchtime, or in the evening. If you choose the evening, be sure to meet as early as possible. You want to be fresh and alert. Don't do it just before bed, because a couple of exhausted, brain-dead spouses can't produce any intimacy.

Where you meet is also important. It must be private and quiet. Send your children to their rooms with strict instructions not to come out until you give them the high sign. Choose a comfortable place like the living room or the den or the back porch. Soft, low lighting will help create the proper ambience. Sit close together like lovers.

I recommend that you not have your couple times in bed. It's too relaxing. Lying down or reclining will make you drowsy. When one partner falls asleep, it kind of ruins the couple time. Besides, the husband may "accidentally" go into fondling mode, and it's hard to fondle and talk at the same time. The bed is for sleeping and sex, not for talking. If you can sit in comfortable chairs in your bedroom, that would work just fine.

Screen out all distractions during these couple times. No television. No computer. No kids. No pets. Don't answer the phone or the door. Do your very best to place all worries and concerns out of reach. You are escaping from the world and all its diversions during this sacred couple time together.

"WHAT DO WE TALK ABOUT?"

I have some excellent material for the two of you to talk about in your couple times. It is well-written, wise, funny, incredibly insightful, and intensely practical guidance on how to do a Marriage Makeover. That's right, I want you to use *this book* in your couple times. I wrote it with this in mind.

Read each chapter, either separately or together. Use your couple times to discuss what you've read and to work through the end-of-chapter Makeover Steps. Take your time and go slowly. Use two or three or even four couple times to cover each chapter. It takes time and several conversations to digest, process, pray about, discuss, and apply each step of the makeover plan.

You are not satisfied with the marriage you have now. You are gathering your support team. You are committed to carving out at least four couple times per week. You're as ready as you're ever going to be for the rest of the Makeover Achievements.

Realization:
"We'd become a family, not a couple."—Brittany

What went wrong?
- First child led to loss of couple time.
- Motherhood, job, and caring for home consumed Brittany's attention.

What's going right?
- Setting aside four nights a week to focus on *The Total Marriage Makeover*.
- Time together talking and praying is creating a better, closer relationship.

Next steps:
- Keep spending time together.
- Keep talking and praying together.

1. How many couple times—using my definition in this chapter—do you have each week? When did you have your last really good conversation?

2. What's keeping you from having couple times? What are the obstacles? Which of the top seven excuses ring true for each of you?

3. Discuss how you plan to do your couple times: where and when. Right now, schedule your minimum of four meetings for this coming week.

4. Commit verbally to each other and in prayer to use this book's chapters as the basis for your couple times.

Chapter 6
Marriage Makeover Achievement 3

BE A GODLY MAN

American culture has some wonderful ideas on how to be a real man and husband. Read this brief list of movie stars and picture the kind of men they have portrayed on screen:

> John Wayne
> Bruce Willis
> Humphrey Bogart
> Harrison Ford
> Robert Mitchum
> Arnold Schwarzenegger
> Clint Eastwood
> Sylvester Stallone

It's an easy exercise, isn't it? These stars have played sensitive, romantic, gentle, and caring men. Men who have shared their feelings openly, without shame or defensiveness. Men who have made it their main goal in life to tenderly meet the needs of the women in their lives. Yeah, right.

These actors have played men who are hard-edged, macho, tough-as-steel, independent, and emotionally distant. The only emotion they've shown is the anger at the enemies they've killed on screen. They don't talk much. They don't bother with romance. They keep their personal thoughts and feelings to themselves. And, through the power of film, they have taught generations of men what manhood is all about. It works in the movies, but it *doesn't work* in marriages.

But it's not just through the movies that culture shapes a man's view of himself. American culture pushes men away from their wives and families by placing a massive emphasis on career success. Newspapers, magazines, and television news shows profile corporate CEOs and entrepreneurs who have huge amounts of power, fame, and money. Most of these men are workaholics who have gone through two or three wives. But who cares? They've made their mark. They're real men.

> *In America, if you're not making serious money in a high-profile, impressive job, you're a loser. A hapless, pitiful loser.*

Most men are insecure because they feel unrelenting cultural pressure to succeed in their careers and provide for their families. Unlike women, who in addition to careers can also define themselves as wives and mothers, men have only their careers to define them. Without adequate relationship skills, men are unable to get their needs met by their wives, children, or friends. And so they're forced to focus on their jobs to get their sense of worth.

Men cover their insecurity by putting up a tough, confident exterior. They talk only about subjects that are superficial and that they feel competent in: work, the stock market, sports, cars, things that need fixing, current events, politics, and the weather. Even when men talk to other men, they say nothing deep or personal. They stick with what they know and feel safe talking about.

FORGET SOCIETY

Husbands, don't look to society for guidance on how to be a man. Society says that you should be good-looking. Financially successful. A sexual superstar. Men, society tells you to think first of yourself because, after all, you're really something special. The way to be happy is to make a ton of money, buy all kinds of male toys, and have sex with as many women as possible.

Is there temporary pleasure in following society's blueprint for male achievement and success? Yes. Does it provide real joy, peace, and fulfillment? Hardly. Take a close look at the icons of male success in business, entertainment, and sports. With commendable exceptions, you'll see lives littered with failed marriages, destroyed relationships, and deeply scarred children.

This is success? I'll tell you what it is. It's stupid. Actually, it's worse than that. It's a lie straight from Satan, the great deceiver. Go ahead and chase society's goals for manhood if you want. When you reach them, you'll find that they're empty pursuits. They have never satisfied. They never will. All they're good for is breaking your wife's heart, damaging your children, and making you miserable.

FOLLOW THE BIBLE

Scripture tells us to love God and be like Christ. The following two verses say it all:

> *"Teacher, which is the great commandment of the Law?"*
> *And He said to him, " 'You shall love the Lord your God with all*
> *your heart, and with all your soul, and with all your mind.' "*
> MATTHEW 22:36–37

> *Therefore be imitators of God, as beloved children; and walk*
> *in love, just as Christ also loved you and gave Himself up for us.*
> EPHESIANS 5:1–2

We are to love God with everything we have and live as Jesus Christ lived. This is the definition of a godly man.

Husband, how does your life match up with this definition? There have been times in my life when I wasn't even close to being a godly man. Oh, I was a Christian, and I was attending church. But I wasn't in love with God, and I wasn't living like Jesus. I was still hanging on to certain areas of sin, and I was living the way I wanted to live. Maybe that's how you're living now. If you can honestly admit that you're not the godly man God wants you to be, then you have some work to do.

YOU WON'T BELIEVE THE BENEFITS

When you love God and walk in a close relationship with Jesus, you have the power to live in the way God has planned. It will make all the difference in your personal life, in your career, and in your marriage relationship.

Because this is a marriage book, I'm going to zero in on that last sentence. The Bible says that God will richly bless the marriage and family of a godly man.

> *Your wife shall be like a fruitful vine*
> *Within your house,*
> *Your children like olive plants*
> *Around your table.*
> *Behold, for thus shall the man be blessed*
> *Who fears the LORD.*
>
> PSALM 128:3–4

Your wife will be thrilled with your spiritual growth. I guarantee it. It's one of the deepest desires—and needs—of every Christian wife. It's tied for first place with—or even slightly ahead of—her need to emotionally connect with you.

> I have heard wife after wife, in my therapy office and at my seminars, tell me, "Oh, I wish my husband were a godly man."

When you're a godly man, your wife will love and respect you in ways you didn't believe possible. You've heard the old saying, "When Momma ain't happy, ain't nobody happy." You know it's true. When your wife isn't happy, it makes you miserable, doesn't it? When you're spiritually healthy, she's happy. Fulfilled. At peace. And she'll feel great about you and turn right around and meet your needs so you'll be happy.

On a practical level, being a godly man will give you the power to be a good husband. Humanly speaking, you can't do it. Not just because women are so hard to live with—although that's true—but because what God requires of us as husbands is so difficult. Have you read Ephesians 5:25 lately? Take a look: "Husbands, love your wives, just as Christ also loved the church and gave Himself up for her."

Whoa! I mean, whoa! How can you love your wife as Christ loved the church—and in your power? No way. I tried to love Sandy in an Ephesians 5:25 way on my own for years, and it didn't work. I finally got past my ignorance and pride and realized that being a good husband is a supernatural job (as is living the Christian life itself). Once I had God's help, I did a much better job of loving Sandy as I should.

> *God knows your woman better than you will ever know her. He knows what she needs. As you get closer and closer to Him, He'll work through you to love her.*

COME TO CHRIST

To be a godly man, you need to know God. And the only way to know God is to know Jesus Christ. Let me give you the straight facts on how to begin a relationship with God through His Son, Jesus.

You are a sinner. So am I. So is everyone. You've made mistakes in your life, haven't you? Well, even one mistake, one sin, separates you from God. On your own, there is no way to reach a holy and perfect God. Romans 3:23 drives this point home: "For all have sinned and fall short of the glory of God."

God could have left you in your sin, condemned to never know Him and to die and go to hell forever. But He didn't do that. God loves you so much that He sent His only Son, Jesus, to earth to die for your sins. Because Jesus paid the price for your sins, you don't have to be eternally separated from God. "For the wages of sin is death, but the free gift of God is eternal life in Christ Jesus our Lord" (Romans 6:23).

First Corinthians 15:3–4 spells out the truth that we must believe in order to know God and to enter His family: "Christ died for our sins according to the Scriptures, and. . .He was buried, and. . .He was raised on the third day."

Do you want all your sins, the ones you've already committed and the ones you will do for the rest of your life, wiped away? Do you want the God-given ability to resist sin? Do you want to know God personally? Do you want God's power to energize your life here on earth? Do you want to go to heaven when you die? If you answered yes to these questions, then you're ready to come to Christ.

Repeat the following prayer to begin a relationship with God (it's not the words that will save you. It is what you are choosing in your mind and heart):

God,
I'm a sinner. I've made mistakes and sinned. I know that my sin separates me from You. I can't reach You on my own. Thank You for sending Jesus as the only way for me to get to know You. I believe that Jesus died on the cross for my sins. I believe that Jesus rose from the dead, proving He is God and has the power to forgive my sins. I'm tired of living my life my way. I now give my life to You, God. Amen.

GROW IN CHRIST

I've seen too many husbands who have come to Christ, who have established a relationship with Christ, but who aren't growing in Christ. I've been there myself, so I'm not throwing any stones. Real men are men who aren't perfect but who are maturing spiritually and growing in their walk with Jesus: "Be on the alert, stand firm in the faith, act like men, be strong" (1 Corinthians 16:13).

If you want to be a real man, be a man who is growing in Christ. Attend church weekly, go to Sunday school, and build relationships with other Christians. Find a place in your church to serve others. Go to a Promise Keepers event—or one of a similar nature—at least once.

Spend time each day alone with God. It can be ten minutes. It can be thirty minutes. It can be early in the morning, at lunch, or in the evening. Talk to God in prayer. Thank and praise Him for what He has done for you and your family. Talk to Him about your life, your feelings, your concerns, and stresses. Ask Him to guide you. Make your requests, but be sure never to make your entire prayer a list of requests.

Listen to God in prayer, too. Through the Holy Spirit, He will find ways to communicate with you. Just be quiet in God's presence and see what happens. The main way God will speak to you is through the Bible. Read a verse or two or a paragraph during every quiet time with God, and meditate on what you read. Every time you read the Bible, God is talking to you.

Reading and meditating on God's Word will lead you to some amazing blessings:

> How blessed is the man who does not walk
> in the counsel of the wicked,
> Nor stand in the path of sinners.
> Nor sit in the seat of scoffers!
> But his delight is in the law of the LORD,
> And in His law he meditates day and night.
> He will be like a tree firmly planted by streams of water,
> Which yields its fruit in its season,
> And its leaf does not wither;
> And in whatever he does, he prospers.
>
> PSALM 1:1–3

BE ACCOUNTABLE TO ONE MAN

Find a godly man who will meet with you once a week face-to-face and will hold you accountable in all the important areas of your life: in your relationship with Jesus, in your role as husband and father, in your career, and in areas of temptation. Very few men have a relationship like this. Be the exception. It will change your life. Moses had Aaron and Joshua. David had Jonathan. Paul had Barnabas. Who do you have?

Over the past seven years, I've had Rocky Glisson. Rocky is my best friend. Unless one of us is sick or I'm out of town speaking, every Saturday morning we sit down in my office for an accountability meeting. We go over the previous week and ask each other the tough questions eyeball to eyeball. I know Rocky's weaknesses, the areas in which he tends to sin, and Rocky knows mine.

Rocky is my supporter, encourager, and confronter. He's the guy I go to war with against Satan, who is scheming to ruin my life. Rocky keeps me away from those sins that will destroy me, my marriage, and my family. One of these areas is work. ("Hello. My name is Dave, and I'm a workaholic.") When Rocky sees me getting carried away, he'll bark: "David, you're in the workaholic zone again. Stop it! Cut back, or I'll have to hurt you." Most important, Rocky keeps me on track spiritually. He asks me how I'm doing in my walk with Jesus. Am I having my daily quiet times? Am I reading my Bible? What did God teach me this week? In every meeting, we share our triumphs, joys, worries, and failures. We end every session by praying for the specific requests we have brought to the table.

Look for a man, your age or older, who loves the Lord

and is an excellent husband. A man who has figured out how to love his wife and meet her needs. A man who has learned how to communicate openly and honestly with his wife. Ask him to teach you how to be a great husband. Rocky has made a huge difference in my life. Because of our accountability relationship, I'm a better husband, father, and psychologist. Best of all, I'm closer to Jesus. Find a Rocky. Start praying and looking. God will lead you to him.

SNAPSHOT
SUSIE AND BOB

The hope:
"The desire of my heart was that you, my husband, would be a godly man."—Susie

What went wrong?
- Bob's commitment to God was primarily outward, only through church attendance.
- Susie struggled to trust Bob, fearful of his lack of spiritual depth.

What's going right?
- Bob recognized Susie's desire for a godly husband.
- Bob began personal quiet time and joined a men's fellowship at church.
- Susie sees Bob as less stressed, slower to anger, happier, and more focused.

Next steps:
- Continue regular Bible reading and prayer.
- Develop marriage as a three-way relationship with God at the center.

1. How macho, independent, and emotionally distant have you been as a man? How much pressure do you feel to succeed in your career? To what degree have you bought into society's blueprint for male achievement and success?

2. How does your life match up with the Matthew 22:36–37 definition of a godly man: "You shall love the Lord your God with all your heart, and with all your soul, and with all your mind"?

3. Do you know God through Jesus Christ in the way I described in this chapter? If not, are you ready to believe by faith that Jesus Christ died on the cross for your sins and rose from the dead?

4. Which of these spiritual growth steps are you willing to take: (1) a daily quiet time with God when you pray and read the Bible, (2) a once-a-week accountability meeting with a Christian man, (3) regular attendance at church and Sunday school with your wife and children, (4) an area of service in your church? Ask your wife how she would feel if you would step forward and follow through on these spiritual behaviors.

Chapter 7
Marriage Makeover Achievement 4

BE A GODLY WOMAN

American culture is trying to "help" wives. Through television, movies, the Internet, newspapers, and magazines, our cultural guides have developed three distinct profiles of the twenty-first-century wife—which, as a public service, I will now describe. Once you've read the descriptions, you can choose which wife you'd like to be.

The first wife is glamorous and physically perfect. Her percentage of body fat is .001. She's so thin, it's scary. She works out a minimum of ten hours per week on her NordicTrack, StairMaster, and ThighMaster. If physical exercise can't give her the body she wants, plastic surgery will. She fights the aging process with every technological advance known to medical science. She dresses in the finest designer clothes, straight from Paris. Her makeup supply would make any supermodel cry jealous tears.

She worships at the altar of the Hollywood Actress Club, that special cadre of magically alluring women who believe they were put on earth to be beautiful and attract desirable men. These anorexically thin, surgically enhanced, botox-injecting, liposuctioning babes spend their lives searching for the right man. They love the intoxicating rush of infatuation and great sex. When the adrenaline surge of lust and excitement wears off—and it always does—they move on to the next man. They're convinced they will eventually find perfect men who will make them happy and make all their dreams come true.

The second modern wife hates men. All men. She believes that men are chauvinistic, arrogant, insensitive, beer-guzzling, sex-crazed, inexpressive, selfish dirtballs. She doesn't trust her husband, doesn't need him, and belittles him behind his back. She'll get rid of him as soon as she can, because his only role is as a sperm donor. Her goal in life is to prove to everyone that she can make it—and make it just fine—without a man.

The third choice offered by American culture is the wife who has a wildly successful career. She tries to get her needs met at work because that's where she spends most of her time. She plays hardball with the big-business boys and always comes out on top. She gives her all to the company, has a corner office with a beautiful view, and is rich and powerful. Incredibly, this workaholic woman also has more than enough time and energy for her children and husband. She masterfully balances her roles of businesswoman, mom, and wife. Her family understands her need to achieve, and everyone is more than satisfied with the limited—but *quality*—attention they receive from her. She shows the world every day that a woman really can have it all.

IGNORE THE WORLD, LISTEN TO GOD

Women, if you attempt to be one of these three culturally approved modern wives, you'll be personally unhappy and unfulfilled and have a rotten marriage. American culture doesn't have a clue about what it takes to be a real wife. Who does? God does. God speaks clearly to wives in the Bible. His principles still apply, and if you obey them, you'll have the best chance for a healthy, intimate marriage. God knows exactly what your husband needs from you. And He hasn't kept this knowledge a secret. Your role as a wife is spelled out in His book.

> To truly touch your husband's heart, follow God's blueprint for a biblical wife.

His blueprint begins with His instruction to be a godly woman.

GOT GOD?

God is the most important person in your life. Others may come and go. Others may let you down. But not God. He will always be with you to give you strength, patience, and endurance. To give you whatever you need. I'm not saying this because it sounds good and because I hope it's true. It's what is written in the Bible:

For He Himself has said, "I will never desert you,
nor will I ever forsake you," so that we confidently say,
"The Lord is my helper, I will not be afraid.
What will man do to me?"

HEBREWS 13:5–6

Who gave Sarah, Abraham's wife, a child when she was more than ninety years old (Genesis 21)? Who protected Jochebed's infant son Moses and allowed her to raise him in his early years (Exodus 2)? Who spared Rahab and her family when all the other inhabitants of Jericho perished (Joshua 6)? Who gave Deborah the victory over Israel's Canaanite oppressors (Judges 4 and 5)? Who brought Ruth from a vulnerable, desperate situation to a life of joy and security with her new husband, Boaz (Book of Ruth)? Who released Abigail from her selfish, rotten, foolish husband, Nabal, and blessed her with her marriage to David (1 Samuel 25)?

Who gave Esther the courage to risk her life and used her to save the Jews from destruction (Book of Esther)? Who raised a widow's son from the dead (Luke 7)? Who healed a woman with a serious internal hemorrhaging condition that no one could treat (Luke 8), and a woman crippled for eighteen years (Luke 13)?

The answer to all these questions is God. All these women were in hopeless situations, and God gave them exactly what they needed most in their lives. God loves the impossible. That's when He does His best work.

"Is anything too difficult for the Lord?" (Genesis 18:14).

"Nothing will be impossible with God" (Luke 1:37).

If God was able to help these women, He can help you. To receive all God's blessings and help, you need to be close to Him. You need to build your faith. You need to be a godly woman.

God always rewards a faithful, godly woman. Always.

Do you want to read a great description of a godly woman? Read these verses: "Your adornment must not be merely external—braiding the hair, and wearing gold jewelry, or putting on dresses; but let it be the hidden person of the heart, with the imperishable quality of a gentle and quiet spirit, which is precious in the sight of God" (1 Peter 3:3–4).

Contrary to almost every message delivered by our culture, God is not interested in what you look like on the outside. He is interested in what you are like on the inside. Your inside is your spiritual life. Your connection to God. Your personal relationship and fellowship with Him. That's what is precious in His sight. That's what He wants you to develop and nurture. In return, God will give you many benefits—some eternal, and many right here and now.

TRUE BEAUTY

Physical beauty fades. No matter how outwardly attractive you are now, you won't stay that way. Everybody gets old. The wrinkles, the gray hair, and all the other indignities of age creep closer every year. And there's nothing you can do about it. Spiritual beauty, however, can improve with age. The most beautiful women I know are in their sixties, seventies, and eighties. They are godly, spiritual women who love Jesus. The inner light of Jesus Christ radiates from them. Now, that's beauty!

THE POWER TO BE A GOOD WIFE

It's not difficult to live with a man. It's impossible! How can you love a man who

- watches ESPN, *Wall Street Week*, the Weather Channel, or some inane sitcom on television instead of talking to you?
- does one three-minute household job and expects the Medal of Honor?
- can come up with only this comment after you've both seen a beautiful, incredibly romantic, heart-breaking movie: "My popcorn was a little stale"?
- thinks he's being Mr. Romantic when he rolls over at 2:00 a.m. for five minutes of passionate, meaningful sex?

The answer is: *You* can't! If you try to love your husband with human strength alone, you'll end up mumbling to yourself in a padded room at the state mental hospital. Or you'll become a bitter, frustrated woman. You can't love your husband on your own, but you and *God* can! With God's help and power, you can continue to love your man and be a good wife to him. As you grow spiritually and stay close to God, you will be living the truth expressed in Ephesians 3:16: "That He would grant you, according to the riches of His glory, to be strengthened with the power through His Spirit in the inner man."

YOUR MOST IMPORTANT NEEDS WILL BE MET

Your husband may not be meeting some of your most important needs: emotional connection, being loved and cherished, true companionship, a spiritual bond, and romance. Even if your husband is doing a pretty good job, it's not nearly enough to fill up your need tank. That hurts. Every day.

Because these God-ordained needs are so important to you, it's very easy to make your number one goal in life getting your husband to meet them. When your efforts fail, you can become even more hurt and devastated. You can begin to believe that your husband is ruining your life. He's keeping you from being happy and fulfilled. He's wasting the best years of your life. He's making you miserable.

Actually, he's not doing any of these things. You're doing them to yourself because you've put your husband at the top of your list of priorities. You've become obsessed with all the things he's not doing for you and all the needs he's not meeting.

It's true that your husband is not meeting some of your most important needs, and you ought to make it your goal to change that situation. That's one of the reasons you're reading this book. But you can't afford to make your husband and his lack of relationship skills the main focus of your life.

There's only one person who belongs on the top of your priority list. There's only one person who can meet the vital needs in your life while you and your husband are in the makeover process. You know who that person is. It is God, your heavenly Father. When you put God first and work on growing closer and closer to Him, He'll keep you from obsessing about your husband. He'll love you, comfort you, and give you a sense of security and *His* joy and peace, a peace that "surpasses all comprehension" (Philippians 4:7). He'll provide powerful spiritual and emotional strength. He'll help you be the best wife, under the circumstances, that any husband ever had.

Take hope in the Word of God as expressed by the apostle Paul: "In any and every circumstance I have learned the secret of being filled and going hungry, both of having abundance and suffering need. I can do all things through Him who strengthens me" (Philippians 4:12–13).

Jesus Himself promises to meet your needs in the midst of difficult, painful circumstances: "Come to Me, all who are weary and heavy-laden, and I will give you rest. Take my yoke upon you and learn from Me, for I am gentle and humble in heart, and you will find rest for your souls" (Matthew 11:28–29).

When your husband does not meet your needs day

after day and month after month, it still hurts. You still suffer, even if you stay close to God. But God will sustain you until your husband changes. If your husband does not change, God will still be there for you.

> God will meet your important needs that a husband cannot meet, deep, profound needs that only He can meet. That's His promise to you.

THE BEST WAY TO BRING ABOUT SPIRITUAL CHANGES IN YOUR MAN

Every Christian wife I have spoken to—every one—has told me that one of her heartfelt desires is for her husband to be a godly man who walks with Jesus and leads her spiritually. Precious few wives have a husband like that. One of the best ways to influence a man spiritually is to model a Christian life that is working. The apostle Peter, a husband himself, wrote these words to Christian wives whose husbands were not living godly lives: "Even if any of them are disobedient to the word, they may be won without a word by the behavior of their wives, as they observe your chaste and respectful behavior" (1 Peter 3:1–2).

Showing your husband, every day, your close, loving relationship with God can have a major effect on his spirituality. It's his responsibility to grow spiritually, but you can help. In fact, you can make all the difference.

I've been married to my beautiful wife, Sandy, for twenty years. For those twenty years and more, her commitment to Christ has helped me grow spiritually. Her influence on my spiritual life actually began when we first met at Point Loma College in San Diego, California. I was the mature, confident sophomore, and she was the shy, starstruck freshman. Okay, I was the awkward, bumbling sophomore who couldn't believe this gorgeous freshman was interested in him.

I was impressed by Sandy's spirituality right away. One of the first places she invited me was to a Bible study in her dorm. I went. I would have gone with her to a tractor pull. Seeing her love for Jesus motivated me to work on my relationship with Jesus, and that's still true today.

COME TO CHRIST

You can't be close to God unless you know Him. You can't know Him unless you know His Son, Jesus Christ. Jesus said, "I am the way, and the truth, and the life; no one comes to the Father but through me" (John 14:6).

The apostle Paul records in 1 Corinthians 15:3–4 what you must believe to become a Christian and establish a relationship with God: "I delivered to you as of first importance what I also received, that Christ died for our sins according to the Scriptures, and that He was buried, and that He was raised on the third day according to the Scriptures."

God loves you so much that He sent His only Son, Jesus, to die to provide forgiveness for all your sins. Jesus died a horrible death on the cross so that your sins would no longer separate you from God. Then, to prove that He is God and has the power to forgive your sins, Jesus rose from the dead. When you believe these truths about Jesus Christ and accept Him as your Savior into your heart and life, you have a permanent relationship with God. You are now His child; He is your Father.

GROW IN CHRIST

Once you know Christ, it is critically important for you to grow in your relationship with Him by continuing to learn about Him and His plan for your life. As you get closer to Jesus Christ, you will also get closer to God the Father and God the Holy Spirit. All three members of the Godhead are vital to your spiritual health.

Spend individual time with Jesus every day. Use this time to talk to Him and listen to Him in prayer. Read and meditate on a Bible passage. Apply what you read in the Bible to your daily life. Pray throughout the day, keeping in close contact with Jesus as you face the challenges and people He brings your way.

Be part of a local church. Listen to the Bible being taught. Build relationships with other Christians. Serve others in the church, using the gifts and talents God has given you.

If you have a husband who is not a spiritual man, do not let him prevent you from growing spiritually. If he tells you not to go to church, tell him that you must follow God's Word, and go anyway. If you have kids, take them with you. If your husband says you may attend church but not get involved in Sunday school or any area of service, tell him that you can't grow spiritually and obey God by merely attending church. Hear him out politely, and then get as involved in your church as God wants you to be, but never neglect your husband or children.

ONE BEST FRIEND

Have you seen *Anne of Green Gables*, the excellent PBS television series about the adventures of a feisty orphan girl who is adopted by a brother and sister in their sixties? The scenery of Prince Edward Island is spectacular. The acting is superb. The story is terrific. Don't tell my male buddies, but I love this series.

One of the most endearing parts of the series is the relationship between the orphan girl, Anne Shirley, and her best friend, Diana Barry. Anne, scared and lonely as she arrives on the island, finds strength and security and love in Diana. They talk together. Laugh together. Cry together. They share their lives—triumphs, trials, and experiences—as only two women can. Anne calls Diana her bosom friend, a kindred spirit.

I believe that every woman (and every man, for that matter) needs a best friend. Like Anne Shirley, you need a female friend who is a kindred spirit. Working to change your marriage is difficult, and you need a buddy to stand with you. To support you. To listen to you when you vent your pain and heartache. To give you godly advice. To pray with and for you. To hold you accountable as a wife and in your areas of weakness.

This friend must be a committed, growing Christian. A woman who will always support your marriage. Someone who can take whatever you say, no matter how intense, angry, or personal, and not freak out and think less of you. She can hear you unload your frustration about your husband and not think less of him. She can keep all your secrets and not tell another living soul, including her husband, what you share with her. She will love you and be there for you. She will also see you as her best friend and use you as her confidante and supporter.

It's ideal to have a best friend who is local. That way she is easily accessible, and your connection to her will be stronger and closer. She also cannot be a family member. A relative is usually on your side and simply cannot be objective. Plus, telling a relative everything about your husband would likely damage his ongoing relationship with the family.

If you don't have a bosom friend like this now, start praying and looking for her. Until you find her, use a long-distance friend or a wise, caring woman at your church. Perhaps one of the pastors' wives or leaders' wives could come alongside you temporarily, though it's possible, of course, that one of these mentor-type women could turn into a great, permanent friend.

Your kindred spirit is out there, in your church, your Bible study, or your neighborhood. In His time, God will lead the two of you together.

The problem:
Mark was a self-confessed "spiritual wimp."

What went wrong?

- Mark was threatened by Janice's close relationship with God.
- Mark shied away from spiritual things, including his relationship with Janice.

What's going right?

- Mark says, "I'm through being a spiritual wimp."
- Spiritual growth has lessened Mark's fear and envy of Janice's relationship with God.

Next step:

- Encourage each other in your spiritual walk.

1. How have you been affected by American society's notions about being a wife? What kind of struggles have you had with your physical body and how you look? Do you have any problems with resenting men and not respecting them? How have you done with balancing a career and your marriage and home life?

2. How do you match up with the 1 Peter 3:3–4 description of a godly woman? "Your adornment must not be merely external...but let it be the hidden person of the heart, with the imperishable quality of a gentle and quiet spirit, which is precious in the sight of God."

3. If you don't know God through a personal faith in Jesus Christ, are you ready now to believe that Jesus died on the cross for your sins and rose from the dead?

4. Which of these spiritual growth steps are you willing to take: (1) a daily quiet time with God in which you pray and read the Bible, (2) a once-a-week accountability meeting with a Christian woman, (3) regular attendance at church and Sunday Bible class, (4) an area of service in your church? Ask your husband how he'd feel if you were to step up and follow through on these spiritual behaviors.

Chapter 8
Marriage Makeover Achievement 5

BE A LISTENER

Husband, what does it mean to be a lover? It's not about sex—which is the first thing that popped into your head when you read the word *lover*. Hey, don't get me wrong. Sex with your wife is important. Very important. In fact, the apostle Paul, under the inspiration of the Holy Spirit, wrote to believers that spouses should not "deprive" one another of this special, wonderful gift from God. I want you to enjoy a regular, passionate sex life with your dear wife.

But being a great sex partner doesn't make you a great lover. In fact, it's just the opposite. Great sex begins and is maintained by your words and your actions throughout the day—*not* just in the bedroom when the lights are out.

> *Being a great lover will make you a great sex partner.*
> *And it will make your wife a great sex partner.*

Now that I have your attention, here's the big idea of this chapter: *A great lover is a husband who meets his wife's emotional needs.* That's the message of the Bible regarding marriage. That's what God wants you husbands to do. Believe me, it's what your wife hopes and prays and dreams you will do. When you learn how to meet your wife's emotional needs, God will shower his blessings on this closest of all relationships that He created. You and your wife will be best friends, you'll be as close and intimate as two persons can be on earth, and your sex life will be nothing short of terrific.

I know you don't know how to be a great lover—*yet.* I didn't know for the first fifteen years of my marriage. I'm going to teach you how. Let's get to it.

EPHESIANS 5 AND THE ONE-TWO PUNCH

Remember Ephesians 5:25? Paul winds up and hits every husband right in the stomach with a dramatic command: "Husbands, love your wives, just as Christ also loved the church and gave Himself up for her." This is the highest possible standard of love! Christ gave everything, including His life, for the church. What you must do is love your wife in the same sacrificial way, totally focusing on meeting her needs.

Paul repeats and amplifies the message with another brutal punch just three verses later: "So husbands ought also to love their own wives as their own bodies. He who loves his own wife loves himself; for no one ever hated his own flesh, but nourishes and cherishes it, just as Christ also does the church" (Ephesians 5:28–29). Your job is to love your wife by *nourishing* and *cherishing* her. By *showing* her the tenderest care and concern just as you do for your own body and just as Jesus does for His church.

It all comes down to your wife's needs. What God, through His servant Paul, is commanding you to do in Ephesians 5 is to meet your wife's needs. The needs that only a husband can meet. Not to *try*, but to *do it*. And some of her most important needs are emotional needs.

LISTEN TO YOUR WIFE

The first step in being a real lover is to learn to listen to your wife. Answer this statement true or false: Men, by nature, are exceptional, excellent listeners. You know the answer, don't you? *False!* Only one man was born a perfect listener: Jesus Christ. The rest of us have to learn. And learn we must if we want to succeed in marriage.

> There isn't a wife in the world who can feel genuinely loved and cherished in an Ephesians 5 way unless her husband listens to her.

All too often, your wife is talking and *you're not listening at all*. You're tuning her out. You're not hearing a word she's saying.

Many men are masters of the ancient and proud art of fake listening. We pretend to be listening to our wives when we're not. All the signs are there: eye contact, leaning forward, nodding the head, a little frozen smile in place.

We even give appropriate-sounding responses: "Yeah." "Really?" "That's fine, honey." "Sure." "Great." "That's nice." The truth is, we have no idea what's being said.

It's fun—until you're nailed. You can't fool a woman for long. Suddenly, with an edge to her voice, she says these five horrible words: "Are you listening to me?" Funny how you always hear that question. You reply, "Yes, of course I am. I'm right here. I'm looking at you."

Then she says the five other words that strike terror in your heart: "What did I just say?" Rats. The jig is up. Now you're in real trouble, buddy. Strike one: You weren't listening to her. Strike two: You lied about it. Strike three: You killed the conversation.

When you don't listen to your wife, communication can't happen. That's obvious. But you also anger and hurt the woman you love. She thinks you don't care about her, because for a woman, *listening* equals *caring*. And if you had any hope of touching her in a special way today, forget it. When she catches you not listening, she won't say, "Man, I love it when you don't listen to me. It drives me wild. Come over here, big boy." I really don't think so. You know what's going to happen. You're going to suffer. And it's your own listening-challenged fault.

Listen to your wife. Focus, reflect, and help her feel understood. If you don't listen to her, she won't feel loved. It's one of her most personal and important needs. Learning how to be a good listener is a big part of being a great lover.

LISTEN TO THE THINGS YOU ARE NOT INTERESTED IN

Your wife talks about many topics you could care less about. But because you care about her and you want her to know it, you must listen and show interest. Here are two examples of industrial-strength listening from my marriage.

Sandy is a crafter, a woman who loves crafts. Sandy makes crafts and buys crafts. She goes to craft stores and craft fairs, and she looks through all kinds of craft catalogs.

You know what I've figured out about crafts? All the craft stores and all the craft fairs and all the craft catalogs sell the same five thousand items. It's all the same stuff no matter where you go! Look, when you've seen one stuffed rabbit holding a wooden heart, you've seen them all. And, believe me, I have seen them all.

It's bad enough to be dragged through all the places that sell crafts, but Sandy also wants to talk to me about crafts. Does this interest me in even the slightest way? No. Do I listen to her? Yes. Why? Because I love her and want to show interest in the things she enjoys.

Frankly, I wouldn't listen to any other woman talk about crafts. I'd just walk away. But for my precious Sandy, I listen. I enter the wonderful world of crafts because that's part of her world. Plus, I want her to listen to my golf stories.

Sandy is also a shopper. Like a lot of women, she enjoys going out on shopping trips—especially to clothing stores. I don't mind her taking these trips. What's tough is listening to her tell me the blow-by-blow account of a three-hour shopping trip. Do you have any idea what it's like listening to this? I'll bet you do. A woman takes five hours to tell you about a three-hour store-hopping adventure. It's the details. The endless, insufferable, tiny details! I don't want to remember that many inconsequential bits of data. But Sandy does, and she wants me to hear them.

I could take it if Sandy just showed me what she bought. That would be fine. But there's a story behind every purchase. There's a story behind every item *almost* purchased. You know: the ones that got away. There's a story behind every store she visited.

The clerk at the Wal-Mart counter is from Boise, Idaho, and Sandy used to have a friend whose boyfriend moved to Boise and really liked it there. It was sad that they broke up, but he started an organic farm and has done well raising cauliflower. Isn't that interesting? No! Not really.

I listen to Sandy's description of her shopping trips because that's what a lover does. When I listen and get involved in her shopping stories, Sandy feels loved. And that's my job: to make her know she is loved and make her feel loved.

LISTEN ACTIVELY

When your wife is talking, what she needs from you is understanding and emotional connection. She's sharing a part of herself with you, and she's hoping you will join her in the experience. When your wife tells you a story, what she's really saying is: "Honey, this is who I am. Relive this event with me, and you'll know me better. And then we'll be closer." The point is not the story itself and the details of what happened. The point is what the story reveals about *her*. That's what she wants—and needs—you to get.

In addition to meeting your wife's emotional needs, active listening is an important survival tool for you. When you listen in passive silence to your wife, a lot of bad things happen. For starters, she thinks you're not listening and will talk more. She'll repeat details over and over, looking for some reaction from you that will indicate you're listening and understanding. You don't want to hear any *more* words, do you?

As her monologue continues, your brain will become overwhelmed and automatically shut down. You'll zone out, get distracted, or fall asleep. Of course, she'll catch you not paying attention and get upset. Then she'll be angry and hurt, and she'll think you're an insensitive jerk who doesn't care about her. The next few hours (at least) will be ruined. You will have blown it, and now you'll pay.

Active listening will take you from mind-numbing monologues to interesting and need-meeting dialogues with your wife. Here's how you do it.

NO DISTRACTIONS

Listening in an active, healthy way to your wife *takes all your attention*. Don't do anything else but listen to her. No television. No computer. No newspaper or magazine. No children. Your only focus is her and what she is saying. You can't even scratch your head while you're listening to the woman. You'll get distracted. You'll find that sweet spot and lose all focus. And your wife will begin to think she'd have a better conversation with the family dog!

Set up the best possible environment for active listening. Sit down with your wife every day for thirty minutes in a comfortable, private place in your home. This is your talk time. It's your job as her husband and lover to make sure these meetings happen. During this thirty minutes, lower the "cone of silence" over your relationship. Without any distractions (you won't even answer the phone or go to the door), you'll have a good chance to be an active listener. We men are highly distractible creatures, so carving out this just-the-two-of-us time is essential.

REFLECT AND ENGAGE

As she talks, look right into her eyes, and feed back verbally her key words, phrases, and emotions. Don't repeat everything she says. Just touch on the highlights and how she *feels* about what she's saying. This selective repetition of content and identification of emotion is called *reflection*. What you're doing is letting her know that you understand what she's saying and feeling.

When she's talking and sharing her story, you say nothing original. It's all about her. You only open your mouth to repeat and rephrase what *she* is saying and the emotional reaction *she* is having about the experience she's describing. Later in the conversation, you can share original thoughts, feelings, and even your famous logic. But not now. In the first part of the conversation, the spotlight is only on her.

The second active listening skill you need to bring to your conversation is *engagement*. You engage your wife by reacting emotionally to her as she speaks. When you reflect, you build understanding. When you engage, you connect with her on an emotional level. To engage is to walk in her shoes and try to feel what she is feeling. As she tells her story, you're reliving the experience with her. Ask her questions about what she is describing. Work to mirror her emotions. If she's angry, you show anger. If she's happy, you get happy and smile. If she's sad and kind of depressed, you show these emotions as well. No one, especially a husband, is perfect at this engagement process. Just do your best; believe me, she'll appreciate it.

HOW AM I DOING?

To learn these active listening skills, you need to have your wife evaluate your progress. During these conversations, ask her how you're doing as a listener. "Do you think I'm getting it?" "Do you feel understood?" "Do you feel connected to me?"

Asking these questions will impress her and make her feel close to you. The feedback she gives you will help you dramatically improve your listening skills. You can make corrections in the same conversation and get back on track. If she tells you that you've missed some content or you're not reacting with enough emotion, just ask her to go over that part of the story again. That won't bother her in the least. In fact, she'll enjoy going over it again.

Let your wife teach you how to listen with reflection and engagement. She is a master of conversational skills. She has been using them her whole life. Swallow your male pride and allow her to guide you in the active listening process. No one else has to know. It will be a secret between the two of you.

When you do a good job as a listener, your wife will talk less. That's a good thing. She'll feel understood. She'll feel loved. Your talks will become much more interesting, stimulating, and revealing. That leads to intimacy. And you'll get drawn into the conversation and get warmed up, which will help you open up and talk when it's your turn.

LISTEN WHEN THERE IS CONFLICT

If you want to be a lover, you're going to have to listen to your wife when she's saying something difficult to listen to. Criticism. Anger. Hurt. Intense negative emotion. Oh, boy. This is beyond tough. She's walking down the hallway and she's coming for you. She has that *look*. You glance behind you, but the door is too far away. You're trapped. Trapped like a mongrel dog. If you're like me, you'll have to fight the impulse to be defensive. Avoid getting angry and firing back at her. Whatever you do, do not ignore her and walk away.

I hate conflict with Sandy. Absolutely hate it. I'll do anything to get out of it. Particularly if I think I'm being unjustly accused. Of course, I always think I'm being unjustly accused.

It's especially important to be an *active listener* when you're in a conflict with your wife and her emotional intensity is spiking. If you do anything else, you're wrong.

- If you use logic and patiently explain how what she's saying doesn't make a whole lot of sense, you're an unfeeling cad—and you're wrong.
- If you raise your voice just a little and express your position, you're mean, and you've hurt her feelings—and you're wrong.
- If you listen but don't say anything, you're not paying attention to her, you don't care about what she's saying—and you're wrong.
- If you tell her this really isn't a good time to be discussing this (the last two minutes of the national championship game; you have a huge work meeting in twenty minutes; it's midnight and you're flat on your back in bed and very drowsy—you name it), you're a selfish bozo—and you're wrong.

Get the picture? When your wife is upset, let her talk. Say *nothing* original until she has fully expressed herself and feels understood. As she points her finger and emotes all over the room, your job is to reflect and engage. You'd better get comfortable, because when a woman is upset, she talks twice as long.

> Don't interrupt a woman when she's on a roll
> unless you want to suffer.

It takes a real man, a courageous lover, to stand in the hurricane and be an active listener. If you can pull this off, your wife will feel understood. She'll calm down. Then *you* can give your view of the situation and she'll be able to listen. Keep in mind that it's always one at a time in a conflict conversation. One partner *speaks* and the other actively *listens*.

SNAPSHOT
SHARON AND STEVE

Realization:
"I noticed you were tuning me out more and more."
—Sharon

What went wrong?
- Steve would "zone out" when Sharon talked.
- Sharon felt rejected and questioned Steve's love.

What's going right?
- Steve is taking steps toward "active listening."
- Four distraction-free, thirty-minute talks each week help Sharon feel understood.

Next steps:
- Keep up regular talking times.
- Maintain the "active listening" steps of reflecting and engaging.

1. Husband, how well do you listen to your wife? On a scale of one to ten (one being lousy and ten being fantastic), rate yourself. Then ask your wife to rate you.

2. What mistakes do you usually make as a listener? What causes you to "zone out" and stop listening or paying attention? Ask your wife how she knows you're not listening in a conversation.

3. Commit to scheduling at least four talk times per week (I hope you've already done this). Schedule those four times *now*.

4. Right now, ask your wife to talk about any topic for five minutes and practice *reflecting* (feeding back to her verbally her key words, phrases, and emotions) and *engaging* (responding emotionally, mirroring her emotions, asking her questions). When she's done, ask her how you did.

5. Commit to practicing your reflecting and engaging skills in your one-on-one talk times over the next month. At each talk time, ask your wife how you did as a listener. Ask her at every meeting what you can do to improve.

Chapter 9
Marriage Makeover Achievement 6

BE SUBMISSIVE

Oh no! The dreaded *S* word! For centuries, submission has been one of the most misunderstood and misinterpreted marital teachings in the Bible. The mere mention of the word can evoke intense, passionate reactions from both husbands and wives. Why? Because submission directly affects every major area in marriage: balance of power, decision making, personal safety and autonomy, communication, sex, finances, parenting. You can name any area of marriage and submission will be an integral part of it.

Wives, my goal in this chapter is to help you understand biblical submission and to take specific steps to do what God wants you to do in this area. You need to be submissive to your husband because that's what God commands you to do. So it is primarily an issue of obedience to God. But it is also an issue of influence. When you submit to your husband, you are using a powerful and God-given tool to motivate him to love you and meet your real needs.

As we ought always to do, let's look at what Scripture says: "Wives, be subject to your husbands, as to the Lord. For the husband is the head of the wife, as Christ also is the head of the church, He Himself being the Savior of the body. But as the church is subject to Christ, so also the wives ought to be to their husbands in everything" (Ephesians 5:22–24). Scripture teaches that the husband is to be in the position of authority and leadership in the marriage relationship. Whenever two or more are gathered in relationship, the need for a leader is created. Two or more cannot all lead. You must have a leader or you will have chaos. God, for reasons of His own, has decided that the husband is to lead his wife.

Being the leader in a marriage is incredibly difficult. Equally difficult is being the one who submits and follows in a marriage. Wives, to help you submit in a healthy, biblical way, I will explain what submission *does not* mean and what it means.

WHAT SUBMISSION DOES NOT MEAN
Submission Does Not Mean That a Wife Is Inferior to Her Husband

God created man and woman for each other. The one-flesh relationship described in Genesis 2:24 is the ultimate picture of perfect unity. To be joined together as one, both must be equal.

In 1 Corinthians 11:11–12, Paul asserts the complete equality of man and woman: "However, in the Lord, neither is woman independent of man, nor is man independent of woman. For as the woman originates from the man, so also the man has his birth through the woman; and all things originate from God." Man and woman fit together in a God-designed, complementary way. Neither is independent of or superior to the other.

In Galatians 3:28 we are given the most powerful and decisive statement possible on the equality of man and woman: "There is neither Jew nor Greek, there is neither slave nor free man, there is neither male nor female; for you are all one in Christ Jesus." We all are equal in Christ. Period.

Submission Does Not Mean That a Wife Should Keep Quiet

All too often, wives are told that submitting means not expressing their opinions and feelings. This message is demeaning, insulting, and not even close to biblical. It is a direct violation of 1 Peter 3:7, which instructs husbands to treat wives with respect. Using submission to choke off a wife's right to expression violates a number of other biblical commands:

"Be devoted to one another." (Romans 12:10)
"Accept one another." (Romans 15:7)
"Serve one another." (Galatians 5:13)
"Bear one another's burdens." (Galatians 6:2)
"Speak the truth in love." (Ephesians 4:15)

Wives, feel free to talk and express yourselves anytime. As if we could stop you. Actually, many husbands do try to suppress their wives' talking, and they use "submission" as their communication-killing rationale. They are dead wrong!

Submission Does Not Mean That a Wife Should Not Have Interests Outside the Home

Two mistakes are commonly made in this area. The first mistake is the view that "a woman's place is in the home." Husbands who hold this position want their wives to focus *only* on keeping house and taking care of the children. "Keep your wife barefoot and pregnant" is their rallying cry. These men are stuck in a 1950s time warp and are not reading the same Bible I'm reading. God does not want wives just to be at home.

The second mistake is our society's view that a successful career should be every woman's number one priority if she wants to be fulfilled. According to this view, work outside the home is always more important, and a woman's career should always come first. Then she can attend to her husband and children and home duties. No, God doesn't think so.

What *does* God think? What does God teach in the Bible about the role of a wife inside and outside the home? He teaches *balance*. In Titus 2:4–5, God, through the apostle Paul, sends this message to wives: "Encourage the young women to love their husbands, to love their children, to be sensible, pure, workers at home, kind, being subject to their own husbands, so that the word of God will not be dishonored." A married woman's primary place of responsibility is the home. Meeting the needs of your husband and children should be your top priority, second only to your relationship with God. If your outside interests or job cause your home duties to suffer, then you are violating Scripture.

Paul is clear about a wife's priorities. However, many wives are able to fulfill their biblical duties in the home *and* be involved in other activities.

> All wives need outside activities and interests to keep from going stale or just plain crazy.

Most husbands have no idea what it's like to be trapped at home all day with children or to work outside the home and also have to work in the home. Ninety-nine percent of husbands wouldn't last one week doing what their wives do week in and week out. These husbands would become quivering, drooling, mumbling basket cases. They'd be taken by ambulance or emergency helicopter to the hospital for drugs, intensive therapy, and observation.

Take a look at the excellent wife of Proverbs 31. Even though she seems a little too good to be true, we can learn from her life. Her focus was undeniably on her household, but she did many other things in her community:

She considers a field and buys it;
From her earnings she plants a vineyard.

Verse 16

She extends her hand to the poor,
And she stretches out her hands to the needy.

Verse 20

She makes linen garments and sells them,
And supplies belts to the tradesmen.

Verse 24

Does this sound like a wife who was chained to her home and didn't venture out into the world? Hardly. Proverbs 31:25 is my favorite verse in this section because it captures the essence of this remarkable woman:

Strength and dignity are her clothing,
And she smiles at the future.

Now that's a wife who made her husband sit up and take serious notice. She was a force to be reckoned with. She had significant influence in her man's life. She was one classy, impressive lady. She was confident, strong, productive, and happy. I'm convinced that a big reason why is that she got outside the home on a regular basis. Her outside activities improved her household and benefited her family. No doubt about it. But they also gave her great, healthy outlets for her creativity and self-expression.

If you are a married woman with preschool children, do not work outside the home unless it is absolutely necessary. Small children need Mom at home. But you must get some time out of the home each week—alone, without the kids. Inform your husband that if you don't get this time off, he'll have a stressed-out, depressed, mean woman on his hands. Tell him: "It'll be continuous PMS, baby! When you look at a pit bull and me, the only difference will be the lipstick!" If he won't help you get away, ask friends, family, neighbors, or fellow church members to stay with your kids. Do whatever you have to do to get regular mental health breaks away from the kids.

Back in the days when we had four small children rambling around our house, Sandy sat me down and told me she needed breaks every week from these little people. We worked out this deal and followed it for years: Sandy would get away from the home every Wednesday from 8:00 a.m. to noon and every Saturday from 9:00 a.m. to 1:00 or 2:00 p.m. and occasionally for evenings out with the girls.

On those few days when I couldn't stay with the kids, we'd get family or friends to help, or we'd hire a babysitter. If a day with the kids had been particularly stressful, Sandy had the option of leaving for a few hours in the evening. She'd meet me at the door when I came home from work and say, "They're all yours, buddy. I'm out of here!" I'd watch her run to the car and peel off in a squeal of burning tires.

Wives, if you have to work outside the home, you have to work. God understands, and He will help. He'll protect your children. Sit your husband down and tell him you need him to be the ultimate team player. Work out a contract that has him doing one-half of the chores and child-rearing duties. Inform him that if you have to work outside the home *and* do most of the household jobs, too, you won't be able to be a very good wife to him. You'll be angry, hurt, and tired.

To make sure you get your husband's attention, tell him that if you are forced to carry the full load at home, your sexual relationship will be a dud. You'll be exhausted and resentful, and you won't be interested in sex. When you do have sex, it'll be just another chore on your list. You'll do it, but you won't be anywhere close to a warm, willing, and responsive partner.

> Tell your husband what you're thinking about during sex after you've killed yourself all evening doing a long list of chores: "Are you through yet?" "Is it over?" "Please, hurry up!"

Submission Does Not Mean That a Wife Must Tolerate Abuse

No, no, no, no. A thousand times no! Wives do not submit to their husbands' physical, verbal, or psychological abuse. Not ever. If your husband is abusing you, he is sinning in an extremely serious way, and God does not want you to submit to sin. God wants you to do just the opposite: stand up, confront his sin, and demand change

(Matthew 18:15–17). We'll cover this topic in greater detail in chapter 11.

WHAT SUBMISSION MEANS

Submission means to allow your husband to be the leader in your relationship and to yield to his authority. Not because he is superior. Not because he is more intelligent. Not because he has more ability. But because this is the role that God commands him to fulfill. Here's how to submit.

Walk Close to God

It is only with God's power, through the Holy Spirit and Jesus Christ working in your life, that you can truly submit. If it's just you in your own power trying to submit, you'll never be able to do it. It's humanly impossible. Submission is a God thing. You submit with God's help, or you don't submit at all. You submit to your husband out of obedience to God. You don't submit for your husband. You submit for God.

> *Wives, be subject to your own husbands, as to the Lord.*
> EPHESIANS 5:22

> *Wives, be subject to your husbands, as is fitting in the Lord.*
> COLOSSIANS 3:18

Don't focus on your husband as you submit. Keep your eyes on the Lord. You're doing it for Him. And He'll bless you for your act of obedience and love.

As An Equal Partner, Speak Your Mind Freely

A critical part of your role as a submissive wife is to openly share your feelings and opinions on significant decisions and issues. Always. God wants you to offer your husband guidance and feedback: "Then the LORD God said, "It is not good for the man to be alone; I will make him a helper suitable for him" (Genesis 2:18). As a helper to your husband, you are to tell him in a loving and honest and firm way what you think is best in every important situation. That's being helpful. That's what a helper does.

Be like the Proverbs 31 wife: "She opens her mouth in wisdom, and the teaching of kindness is on her tongue" (v. 26). You have wisdom that no one else has about your husband, your children, and your home. You need to share that wisdom. Your husband may not always want to hear what you have to say. That's too bad. Lay it on him anyway. That's your job. That's obeying the Lord and following His plan.

Let Your Husband Lead

Allow your husband to make decisions in the key areas of life, and follow them unless they clearly violate God's revealed will. Fully share your views about a situation, talking a number of times over several days to several weeks if you're making a major decision. Pray together about the decision. And then allow your husband to decide what to do, and support him and the approach he wants to take, whether you agree or not.

Husbands, the only time your decision should run counter to your wife's opinion and feelings is when you can honestly say something like this: "Honey, I have thought long and hard about this. I have prayed continually for God's guidance. I've read whatever I can that the Bible says about this. I've listened thoroughly to you and your feelings and ideas. I've asked a couple of good and godly men about their experience and for their opinions. As far as I can discern, I believe this is what we should do."

Wives, if your husband is sinning, do not submit. Confront his sin and take action against it. If he asks you to do something that would go against biblical principles, do not submit. Refuse to sin for him.

If your husband is too harsh with the kids, step in to protect them, and confront his sinful behavior. If he is financially irresponsible, confront that sin and take steps to bring about repentance. If he says you can't go to church, go anyway. If he asks you to sign a fraudulent income tax form, refuse to sign it. Whatever the circumstance, confront sin in accordance with Matthew 18:15–17:

> "If your brother sins, go and show him his fault in private; if he listens to you, you have won your brother. But if he does not listen to you, take one or two more with you, so that by the mouth of two or three witnesses every fact may be confirmed. If he refuses to listen to them, tell it to the church; and if he refuses to listen even to the church, let him be to you as a Gentile and a tax collector."

If your husband is involved in serious sin, you will need to lean heavily on your support team. Your team is there to help you apply the Makeover Achievements. Your team is also there to provide practical, hands-on assistance when you are in a crisis situation with a sinning husband.

If you need to confront a sinning husband, do not go it alone. Tell your accountability partner, your mentor couple, and your pastor what is going on and hold a meeting in which you and your team members pray and discuss the steps you will take. If your husband has a temper and is prone to violence, it is even more important to lean on your team members and move as a group carefully through the steps of confrontation. You will find more on how to specifically confront an abusive spouse in chapter 11.

The Proverbs 31 wife did many, many things on her own—for the good of her husband and children and home. The truth is, you can and should make many decisions on your own: about child care, groceries and other purchases, discipline of the children, many home-related areas, personal life, and more. But on major issues, the husband ought to chart the course and be responsible for making the decisions.

> *Most of the time, when the two of you talk and pray, you will agree. But sometimes you won't, and when that happens, the husband must make the call. He's the leader. That's his job.*

Over the twenty years of my marriage, I've made some good decisions. And I've made some bad decisions. I mean, some real duds! "What was I thinking?" decisions. Leaders make mistakes. Wives, please follow the example of my long-suffering wife, and don't say, "I told you so!" That's not nice, and it's not submissive.

What If He Refuses to Lead?
If your husband refuses to lead in a biblical way, submission is a moot point. You don't submit to him. Why? Two reasons:

1. There can be no submission if there's no leadership. You literally cannot submit to a man who isn't leading. There's nothing to submit to.
2. He is in violation of Scripture and is therefore sinning. You do not submit to someone who is sinning. You can and should confront that sin according to Matthew 18:15–17.

If your husband is not a leader, then *you* will have to lead the family. It's not God's Plan A, but you really have no choice. You will lead family devotions. You will make sure home repairs get done. You will make financial decisions. You will guide your children's lives. When your husband crabs about your leadership, tell him you'll step aside as soon as he assumes his God-ordained position as head of your marriage and family. Perhaps my Marriage Makeover strategy will help motivate him and teach him to step up and be your leader.

SNAPSHOT
GARY AND DENISE

Realization:
"I'm sorry for my mediocre-to-poor leadership as a husband." —Gary

What went wrong?
- Gary has made poor decisions, sometimes apart from Denise.
- "Dropping the ball" has forced Denise to take charge at times.

What's going right?
- Denise has made an effort to be submissive and support Gary's decisions.
- Gary wants and invites Denise's input on decisions.
- Gary invites Denise's constructive criticism.

Next steps:
- Denise: Continue submitting to Gary's leadership.
- Gary: Continue to honestly seek out Denise's input.

1. Wives, what do you think of when you think of *submission*? What have you been taught—at home and at church—that it means? How did your mother act with regard to submission to your father?

2. Which lies about submission have you believed? Who taught you these lies?

3. If you need more time outside the home (and who doesn't?), tell your husband how many hours per week you need, and figure out a schedule. Talk to him about what you'd like to do with this time.

4. What is the most difficult thing about submission for you?

5. Ask your husband how you're doing in the area of submission. Tell him what he can do to make submission easier for you.

Chapter 10
Marriage Makeover Achievement 7

BE A TALKER

Most men are lousy communicators—at least with their wives. I am—or at least I used to be. As men, we hold our thoughts and feelings inside and don't talk personally with our wives. Ring any bells? This ingrained style of not letting anyone, especially our wives, see who we really are inside is bad for us and for our marriages.

I know you love your wife. You love her more than anyone else on this earth. But she needs to hear you talk in order to understand your love for her.

> *If you're not talking regularly with your wife on a personal level, I have some bad news for you: She doesn't feel loved by you.*

The number one desire of your wife's heart is to be close to you. To know you as no one else knows you. To hear you talk honestly and openly about your life, your work, your relationship with her, your walk with God, your children, your hopes and dreams, her life, and the things that are important to her.

She wants you to join her in building a better, closer, and deeper relationship. She understands that what she's asking will be very difficult for you. In fact, it will be one of the most difficult things you have ever done. But she is hoping and praying that you love her enough to do it.

For years I held back with my wife, Sandy. I talked with her only about safe, superficial topics. She tried over and over to get me to lower my wall and let her see what I was really thinking and feeling. But I wouldn't do it. I didn't think she needed to know the personal things about me. Man, was I wrong.

I was hurting her deeply! I was making my precious wife unhappy and unfulfilled in our marriage. It was *my fault*. Hiding behind my wall and holding her at arm's length was squeezing the life out of her and our marriage. We still loved each other, but we weren't feeling or acting in love. The fun, the romance, the exciting sex, and the passion were gone. Maybe that's where you are now.

I finally figured out how to open up and let Sandy see inside. To know the real me. I won't lie to you. It wasn't easy. But it has been worth all the effort. Sandy and I are closer and happier now than we've ever been. Our marriage has taken off. And it all started with my understanding Sandy's needs. I thought I knew her needs, but I didn't have a clue. I did three things to figure out exactly what she needed. I talked to her many times, I listened to thousands of wives in my therapy office tell me what they needed from their husbands, and I studied the Bible.

Do you know what I discovered? Sandy's expressed needs, and the needs that all these wives mentioned, were the very same needs that God describes in the Bible. One of your wife's top needs is for you to learn to talk to her on a personal, revealing level.

> God knows your wife intimately. He knows what she needs. If you follow His instructions·about how to be a good husband, you will meet your wife's most important needs.

YOU HAVE TO TALK TO HER

Listening is crucial, but it's not enough to meet your wife's emotional needs. To be an Ephesians 5:25 husband, you also have to *talk* to her. And I don't mean just safe, superficial talk, reporting facts about your job, current events, finances, the kids, and sports. That won't do your wife or your relationship any good. She can talk to the lawn-care man about those topics.

I mean deeper, more personal talk. What do you think and feel *inside* about the events of your day? What are you worried about? What's going on in your relationship with her, the kids, and others close to you? What are your hopes and dreams and goals? How are you doing in your walk with Christ? These are the topics your wife desperately wants you to share with her.

You say, "Dave, I'm just not a talker." That is a big, fat cop-out. I know, because I used that line for years with Sandy. What you're saying is, "I'm choosing not to meet one of my wife's most basic needs. As a result, she'll be

unhappy and feel unloved for the rest of our marriage."
When you were single, you didn't have to talk on a personal level with a woman. That was fine, but you're no longer single. *You* married this woman, and now you have to learn to talk to her. You're not ever going to talk as much as she does. Don't worry. You may never have her volume of words or her emotional intensity. But you can work your way to the place where you talk enough so she feels loved. So she feels close to you.

I've helped thousands of husbands learn how to talk personally with their wives. Now I'm going to help you if you want help. (Desire is an indispensable element.) Here are my top ten talking strategies for husbands.

One-On-One Talk Times
I covered this strategy in chapter 5, but it bears repeating. Husbands, it's your job as the leader of your marriage to initiate and maintain a minimum of four one-on-one talk times each week with your wife. If you can get in five, six, or seven talks, that's even better. These will be twenty to thirty minutes in length and will take place in a private, quiet, and comfortable place in your home. If you don't create regular talk times, the rest of my strategies won't work for you.

The Pad
Prepare for your daily talk with your wife by carrying a notepad with you everywhere you go. Just get one of

those small writing notebooks you can find in any drug-store. As you go through your day and things happen to you that you think might interest your wife, jot them down. It might be something that made you feel an emotion like anger, frustration, or happiness. It might be an interaction with another person. It might be something God taught you.

When you get home and meet with your wife in your one-on-one talk time, you'll have a little list of things to share with her. Don't trust your memory. You don't have a memory! Your wife remembers everything. You remember nothing. Use the Pad. (For more help with using the Pad, see chapter 5 in my book *Men Are Clams, Women Are Crowbars*.)

I've had many husbands say to me, "Dave, I'll feel like an idiot going around all day with my Pad and then sitting in front of my wife with it." My response has always been the same: "You'll feel like a bigger idiot when you're sitting in front of your wife with nothing to say."

Share Work Stress

Of all the husbands I've seen in therapy, 99.9 percent have told me, "I leave work at work. I don't talk to my wife about what goes on at my job. Rehashing my work day will make me miserable and stress me out." I'll tell you what I've told these husbands: "Although it is a natural tendency to stuff your work stress, it's not healthy for you or for your marriage. Unless you work for the

CIA and have to keep secrets for national security reasons, you need to talk with your wife about problems at work. When you open up and express your work stress with your wife, it will lower your stress level and bring the two of you closer."

Graveyards are filled with husbands who stuffed their work stress and kept it buried in their guts. Sure, they checked out early with heart attacks, strokes, and other deadly, stress-related traumas, but at least they held the line and kept work at work. If you want to live healthier and longer, regularly talk out your work stress with the one person you love and trust more than anyone else on earth.

Just recently I had a husband in my office who finally realized the futility and danger of keeping his work life a secret. This guy had hypertension, chest pains, and headaches from stuffing his job stress for twenty years. He was a heart attack waiting to happen. When he followed my advice and took the risk of sharing his work stress with his wife, do you know what happened? The same thing that's happened with every husband who began cleaning his system of work-related strain, tension, and pressure with his wife. He felt relief and a significant reduction in his stress level. His chest pains and headaches went away. He felt better than he had in years.

His wife felt better because she got to know him better. His job was a huge part of his life that he had walled off from her. She wanted and *needed* to know what was going on at work and the problems he was facing. She couldn't solve the problems, but she could listen and be a valuable source of support and encouragement.

Was their marriage better and closer because of his decision to talk about work? You'd better believe it. He said to me: "Dave, I wish I'd done this twenty years ago." All I could say was: "Better late than never. Most husbands never get it."

Debrief

After a government agent returns from an important mission, he is taken to a private, secure location to be debriefed. This means he talks through all the aspects of his mission, placing special emphasis on the more critical details of his assignment. In the same way, you and your wife need to debrief after events in your lives.

When you return from an event in which you were involved alone—whether it was happy or sad, delightful or stressful, a day at work, a meeting at church, a sporting event with a buddy, a business trip, or a social gathering—sit down with your wife and debrief. Using the notes you jotted down on your Pad, tell her what happened and how you felt about it. She needs to know what the experience was like for you. She'll give her own responses to what you'll share, and you and your life mate can dialogue your way to an intimate connection.

When the two of you are leaving an event you attended together, start debriefing in the car. Continue debriefing at home. Tell your wife your impressions, what was most meaningful to you in the experience, and the emotions that were triggered.

Don't say what most husbands say: "It was okay." "Pretty good." "I don't know." These responses are fine if you're talking to one of your male buddies. But not when you're communicating with your wife. Debriefing means digging deeper and expressing your emotional reaction to these shared events.

For example, be prepared to debrief after watching a movie with your wife. Don't bother going to a movie with her if you're not willing to fully discuss it afterward. That's the whole point! It's not about the movie; it's about the intimacy you can create by talking about the movie. I could say the same thing about any event you go to alone or together. In fact, I *will* say the same thing: it's not about the event; it's about the intimate connection you can create by talking about the event.

Your Pool of Memories
Sadly, your short-term memory is shot. You can't remember what happened today unless you write some significant details on your Pad. Your long-term memory, however, is just fine. You have a huge pool of memories that stretch back for years. Childhood. Family vacations. Junior high and high school. College years. Young adulthood. Dating. All the events in your marriage and your family life.

A current event will trigger a memory. Each memory

has emotions attached to it. If you share this memory with your wife, it can lead to a stimulating, deeper conversation. If you're with your wife and a memory is triggered, share it on the spot. If you're not with her, jot the memory on your Pad and share it with her later.

Your Past Pain

The past pain category of conversational material isn't pleasant, but it can generate some serious intimacy. Talking with your wife about painful events in your past, resolved or unresolved, will open a window to who you really are—and some reasons why. Something in the present—a movie, a song, a certain smell, a stressful event—will trigger a painful memory. Don't respond like a typical male and stuff it down deep. Choose to bring it out into the open with your precious wife.

Your Spiritual Life

Who knows how you are doing spiritually? Who knows what your relationship with Jesus is like day-to-day and week-to-week? No one. Am I right? Your wife, your one-flesh partner, has a right to know. When you regularly share with her what is happening in your spiritual life, you will meet her need to know who you really are.

This is the most personal and intimate information about yourself. I understand that. But that's the point of a one-flesh relationship.

> *Letting your wife know the details of your spiritual journey will require faith and courage. But if you want a personal and intimate marriage, you must do it.*

Use a few minutes of each one-on-one talk time to share with your wife how you're doing spiritually. Tell her what God communicated to you through the pastor's sermon on Sunday. How your daily quiet times with God are going. What God is teaching you through your Bible reading, life events, and prayer times.

Speaking of prayer, pray with your wife during your talk times. I recommend starting with three brief prayers per week. Each of you pray out loud, one at a time, for a total of five minutes. Create a list of prayer requests: your marriage, your children, family members, friends, your pastor and the ministries of your church, health concerns, job issues, and so on.

God will bless you for sharing spiritually and praying with your wife. Your wife will bless you with respect, love, and admiration. The two of you will experience the deepest times of intimacy possible.

Let Her Ask Questions

Your wife is a curious person. She wants to know everything about you and what's happening in your life. She believes—and she's right—that the more she knows about you, the closer she will be to you. To gather information, she asks you questions. Many, many questions.

Many, many, many questions.

Husband, your job is to let your wife ask her questions and to answer them. Don't let your natural response of defensiveness and feeling pressured get in the way. Keep in mind that she is not a foreign counterterrorism agent torturing you for information. I know it can seem that way, but it isn't. She is your dear wife, and she longs to know who you are. That's why she asks questions.

As a man, you need help to bring out your emotions and personal reactions. Let her questions help you.

Build in some boundaries to make these question-and-answer sessions go more smoothly. Let your wife know if she is asking too many questions too rapidly and causing you to get overwhelmed. If you need a break, take a break, and then you can resume the interrogation—I mean *conversation*.

Extend Your Conversations

True conversational intimacy never happens in just one sitting, in one conversation, about a topic. It happens over the course of several conversations over several days. Most husbands don't understand this key talking strategy. They talk briefly about one topic with their wives and then drop it. It never comes up again

If you want to please your wife and meet her need for closeness, you have to learn to extend your couple conversations. Let's say that today the two of you talk about this past Sunday's sermon. The topic sparks some interest, and you spend five or ten minutes discussing your responses to it. To gain a deeper level of intimacy, bring up this same topic (the pastor's sermon) again in tomorrow's couple time and talk about it some more. Talk about it again in your next two couple times. You'll get deeper each time you discuss the same topic.

Whatever the topic of interest, talk about it two, three, or four times over two, three, or four days. Between talks, write your thoughts and reactions on your Pad. In this way, you will squeeze every ounce of intimacy out of the topic and experience real emotional connection.

If Necessary, See a Counselor

If these nine talking strategies don't seem to be opening you up, and you're still struggling with expressing yourself with your wife, you may need some extra help. See your pastor or a Christian therapist and ask for specific guidance in this critical area. It's not easy to take this step, but it could make all the difference in your marriage. If you can't talk personally with your wife, your marriage will never be great. It may not even get to be good.

A trained, experienced Christian counselor can help you identify and remove the obstacles that are preventing intimate conversation with your wife. There are reasons why you can't share personally. With some digging, and some hard, perhaps painful, work, these reasons can be found and resolved.

SNAPSHOT
JENNY AND DAVID

Realization:
"You just wouldn't talk to me!"—Jenny

What went wrong?
- Sit-down talks were infrequent and superficial—discussing bills, kids' activities, and the like.
- Jenny put pressure on David to talk more, causing him to withdraw more.

What's going right?
- David has scheduled regular talk times with Jenny.
- David uses a notepad to record personal items for discussion.
- Conversations are turning toward spiritual things.

Next steps:
- Maintain regular discussion times—four to five per week.
- David: Continue to use a notepad for discussion starters.

1. How much personal, deep, revealing conversation do you have with your wife? Ask her to comment on this.
2. What—in your past, personality, and life—blocks you from opening up and sharing on a more personal level? Is your wife inadvertently doing things that stop you from opening up?
3. Which of my top ten talking strategies are you willing to put into practice? Choose three right now that you will immediately—this week—begin.
4. Commit to asking your wife once a week how you're doing as a talker. Believe what she says, and be willing to follow any suggestions she makes. Remember, she is your loved one, and you want to talk in ways that make her feel loved.

Chapter 11
Marriage Makeover Achievement 8

BE WORTHY OF RESPECT

Wives, what kind of woman does God want you to be? Examine these biblical examples, and you'll get a clear picture of what God is looking for in your life.

NOW, THAT'S A WOMAN!

Sarah, who was so far past childbearing age that it wasn't even funny, trusted God to give her a child. She assertively spoke her mind with her husband, Abraham. She remained at Abraham's side through many trials and painful circumstances.

Miriam was tough enough to speak directly to Pharaoh's daughter and offer to get a nurse for her baby brother, Moses. That nurse was their own mother. Miriam helped lead the Israelites, serving as a key aide to Moses.

Rahab hid the Israelite spies right under the noses of the Jericho authorities. She risked everything because of her faith in God and her desire to protect her family.

Abigail was a strong, intelligent woman married to

an evil man, Nabal. She prevented the slaughter of her entire household by going behind her husband's back to give David and his men provisions. With clear and persuasive words, she convinced David to back away from violence. She helped God's man, David, and had the guts to tell Nabal what she had done.

Deborah ruled Israel with wisdom, strength, and decisive action. She did not hesitate to tell her chief general, Barak, what she thought of his weak response to God's battle command. She went to war and brought peace to Israel for forty years.

Ruth endured the loss of her husband and refused to stay in Moab. She remained loyal to her mother-in-law, Naomi, and to God.

Esther risked her life to stand against evil and save her people, the Jews. It wasn't her great beauty that defined her. It was her character and her courage.

The Proverbs 31 wife was industrious, creative, confident, resourceful, caring, wise, and strong. Best of all, she loved God. She was the bedrock of her marriage and family.

Mary, the mother of Jesus, was caught in a crisis situation that was not her fault. Squeezed by tremendous pain and stress, she did the right thing. She did what God asked her to do. She gave birth to the Savior and raised Him.

Mary Magdalene loved Jesus with her whole heart. She didn't let her past sins or the criticism of others stop her from serving her Lord faithfully.

Priscilla was the excellent wife of Aquila and a prominent member of the early church. She worked alongside the apostle Paul in making tents. She risked her life for Paul. Along with Aquila, she confronted the orator Apollos and corrected his teaching.

Wow! These women were amazing, weren't they? Strong. Courageous. Assertive. Dignified. Women of character. Women of influence. Women of action. Women who were warriors in God's army. Women who spoke the truth without fear and without apology. Women who were willing to take a stand for themselves and for God.

As I read their stories in the Bible, it struck me that all these dynamic women shared one essential quality: respect. They earned the respect of everyone who knew them. They were particularly respected by the men in their lives. It was respect that gave them the ability to influence others in positive, godly ways.

God wants you to have the same respect that these biblical women enjoyed. When you are a woman—a wife—who has respect, you will have what it takes to be a truly biblical wife.

When you have respect, you will get your husband's attention and keep it. You will influence him and motivate him to be the best husband he can be.

BE A 1 TIMOTHY 3:11 WIFE

"Women must likewise be dignified...." First Timothy 3:11 puts into words what these biblical heroines had and what God wants you to have: dignity. The New

International Version uses the phrase "worthy of respect."

Paul is speaking here to the wives of church leaders. Just as these wives needed respect to serve effectively in the local church, so do all wives need respect to serve effectively in their marriages.

Let's take a look at some practical ways in which a woman can be a wife worthy of respect.

CONFRONTING AN ABUSIVE HUSBAND

Do not ever tolerate abuse from your husband. To allow yourself to be treated with such lack of respect is tremendously dangerous to you and to your husband. You suffer a loss of dignity and are emotionally traumatized. You will be depressed, feel worthless, and be unable to carry out your biblical role in the home. Loving confrontation gives your husband the opportunity to stop the abusive behavior.

> *It is not God's will for you to allow behavior that harms you, your husband, your marriage, or your children.*

I recommend—and God requires—a strong, tough love response to abuse. Abuse is sin and therefore must be confronted head-on, according to the pattern set out in Matthew 18:15–17:

> *"If your brother sins, go and show him his fault in private; if he listens to you, you have won your brother. But if he does not listen to you, take one or two more with you, so that by the mouth of two or three witnesses every fact may be confirmed.*

If he refuses to listen to them, tell it to the church; and if he refuses to listen even to the church, let him be to you as a Gentile and a tax collector."

Physical Abuse

If your husband has physically abused you in any way—hitting, kicking, shoving—take your kids and get out of the house *immediately*. Call the police and get a restraining order against him. (If you feel you are in any danger, take all precautions and do not rely on a restraining order. Be warned that a restraining order can easily be violated.) Press charges of domestic violence and force him to face the full extent of the legal consequences of his actions. You won't break the pattern of violence any other way. Staying with a man who has been physically violent is not only enabling him, it's dangerous. *Any* touching whatever that is not gentle and loving has no place in marriage. Ever.

An Affair

If your husband is involved in an affair and refuses to stop, get him out of the home. Kick him out! With the help of a few friends, pack up all his clothes and personal items in garbage bags. Call him and say: "Until you stop your affair, confess, and repent, and prove real change, I don't want you living in this home. I've packed all your stuff, and it's in the driveway. Come and pick it up. You'd better hurry—it looks like rain."

Psychological Abuse

Maybe your husband is psychologically abusing you. Are you living with an alcoholic? A man addicted to drugs? A man who flies into rages and screams at you and the kids? A man who regularly criticizes your weight, your housekeeping, your mothering skills, and other areas of your life? Shun this kind of man. Don't talk to him. Don't have sex with him. Don't do his laundry, cook food for him, or run errands for him.

Stop Submitting to Sin

Don't submit to sin and thereby enable it. As God makes clear in Matthew 18:15–17, we are to resist and confront sinful behavior. Confront sin. Fight sin. Pull away from sin. These biblical actions protect you and your children. God doesn't want you to be destroyed by your husband's sin. Your tough love may get his attention and motivate him to come back to God and change.

God's goal is always restoration of the relationship, but that can happen only if sinful behavior changes. Your husband won't change unless he has to. When he realizes he has lost you, maybe he will break and do whatever it takes to win you back.

If you do nothing, your husband won't suddenly wake up one day and change. You know what he'll do? He'll keep on abusing you until there's nothing left of you, the children, or the relationship.

Abuse Demands Four Steps

Are you living with an abusive husband? If you are, there are four steps you need to take. First, gather your support team and get everyone on board for the confrontation process. You can't do this alone; it's too tough. Call a meeting, without your husband's knowledge, of your entire team: your accountability partner, your husband's accountability partner (if you trust this man completely and know he will support you 100 percent), your mentor couple, and your senior pastor or one of the associate pastors. At this point, I would also add to your team one or more of your family members.

Prior to the meeting, tell each team member—by phone or in person—exactly what your husband is doing. Hold back no details. Make sure each member is willing to support you through the entire confrontation process. Any member who acts squeamish and undecided about the need to confront will not be invited to the meeting. You only keep those members who are ready to stand with you against your husband and his sin.

At the meeting, all of you will discuss your husband's sin and plan the steps of confrontation. Read Matthew 18:15–17 out loud and pray that God will use these intervention steps to cause your husband to repent and change.

The second step is to stand up to your husband and demand to be treated with respect. This may take you awhile if you are used to being passive. Get angry with a righteous anger (Ecclesiastes 3:5, 8; Ephesians 4:26), and stay angry until you have taken all these steps. Keep in regular, frequent contact with your support team. Though I am aware of the reasons why some women will endure abuse, it is amazing to me what some wives will put up with from their husbands. I'm saying, and I fervently believe God is saying, you don't have to put up with it anymore.

Third, pull back from the abuser emotionally and physically. Stay back until he shows evidence of genuine change. Forget his promises. He has promised a million times and always gone back to his sin, hasn't he? This time, require positive action sustained over time. This time, require Christian counseling and serious spiritual growth.

Fourth, follow the Matthew 18:15–17 steps. Begin these steps even if he shows some signs of repentance:

1. Confront your husband one-on-one. If you fear any kind of an intense reaction, go through the confrontation with one or more of your support team members with you.
2. If that doesn't work, go back with one or two witnesses (support team members) and confront him again.
3. If that doesn't lead to repentance and clear action to change, go to the leaders of your church and ask them to do an intervention.
4. If that doesn't work—if he still refuses to repent and begin a whole program of change—shun him in your home for one month. Ignore him and act as if he doesn't exist. Perform no service for him. Say nothing to him.

5. If shunning doesn't work, make plans to physically separate.

Again, throughout this entire confrontation process, lean on your support team members. They are bearing your burden (Galatians 6:2) and giving you the strength and practical help you desperately need. (For a complete, detailed description of how to apply the principles of Matthew 18:15–17 to a sinning spouse, see my book *What to Do When Your Spouse Says "I Don't Love You Anymore."*)

I hope and pray that you are not being abused. If you are not, it is still very possible that you know someone who is being abused by her husband. Or it could even be the wife abusing the husband. Please share this information with this person and support her or him in the confrontation process.

EARNING THE RESPECT OF A NONABUSIVE HUSBAND

Even if your husband isn't abusing you, it's still important to be worthy of respect. You need to command respect as a wife. If you don't have your husband's respect, he may not abuse you, but he will mistreat you. He won't be attentive. He won't open up and talk personally with you. He won't meet your needs. He won't love you the way you want and need to be loved.

> *When respect goes down, love goes down. If you behave like a doormat, the finest man in the world may wipe his feet on you. And the crazy part is, he won't even know he's doing it. It's human nature.*

There is one central way to earn the respect of a non-abusive husband.

One-Way Communication

You gain and keep your husband's respect by being upfront, honest, and completely straightforward, using one-way communication. One-way communication is going directly to your husband and *briefly* telling him the truth, your emotions and thoughts, about something that has happened in your relationship. I call it one-way because *you* do all the talking.

Tell your husband that he doesn't have to respond. Ask him to listen and concentrate in order to understand; let him take time to process what you've said; and when he's ready, ask him to find you and share his reaction. When you're done talking, simply stop. Go silent. If you're at home, walk away. If you're in the car, at a restaurant, or out somewhere, just be quiet for at least five minutes. You can continue in silence or bring up another topic of conversation.

Speak your piece and move on. Unlike what you've done in the past, do not press him for an immediate reaction. Why not? Two reasons:

1. Men cannot respond right away. They need time to process and figure out their feelings and thoughts on an issue. When it's a personal issue, it takes them even longer.
2. Men will always clam up when they feel pressured by a woman. They feel controlled, and they show you with their silence that you can't make them talk.

If you express yourself in two minutes or less and allow your husband time to process, there is at least a chance your husband will consider what you say and get back to you to continue the conversation. If you badger him, or even ask him nicely for a quick response, he will harden up and never respond on that topic. Never. My way, the one-way communication strategy, gets you a *maybe*. Your way, the natural female way of pushing him to respond right away, gets you a *never*. Do it my way.

Do the Two-Step When He Doesn't Return to Talk
What if you employ the one-way method and your husband still doesn't come back to you with a response? Well, he is a man, and that's certainly going to happen a lot. When you have waited a day or two and it's pretty clear he has no intention of giving you a response to your statement, take two steps:

Step One: Give him one—and only one—low-key, nonemotional reminder. If you remind him twice, you're nagging. Say these words: "Remember that issue we discussed? When you're ready, I'd like you to find me and give me your reaction to what I said." After you've uttered these two statements, say nothing else about it. Move on.

If he still won't talk about it, go to Step Two.

Step Two: Go to him and give him a one-way communication that expresses your feelings about his decision to ignore you and refuse to respond to the topic. It'll go something like this: "I'm angry and disappointed that you've chosen not to come back to me about [name the issue you brought up]. It makes me feel unloved and unimportant. I just wanted you to know." Then drop it and walk away. Don't bring it up again.

The Seven *Keeps* of One-Way Communication

There are many benefits of one-way communication. I call these the Seven *Keeps*:

- It *keeps* your system clean of negative, destructive emotions like anger, hurt, bitterness, and resentment. You get rid of the pain your husband has caused you, and you stay emotionally, physically, and spiritually healthy.
- It ensures that you *keep* on forgiving your husband for the mistakes he makes. You have to continue to flush out your daily pain. If you don't, it will turn into resentment and you will develop a nasty pool of negative, debilitating emotions.
- It *keeps* your needs and the behaviors that bother you in full view before your husband. Every time you vent one-way, you remind him of the things

you consider most important in the marriage.

- It *keeps* him off balance and uncomfortable, and that's the only time he'll change.
- It provides you the opportunity to *keep* teaching your husband the skills he needs to love you and express this love: how to correct his weaknesses, how to understand why he is the way he is, how to stop hurting you, and how to open up and communicate what's inside him.
- It *keeps* alive the possibility that he'll actually listen to you, "get" what you're saying, think about it, and give you a response—at least, some of the time. When you drop your verbal payload—not angrily, but honestly—and leave, he may eventually follow you. He doesn't like it when you're upset with him, so he's likely to come after you.
- Most important, it *keeps* you following Scripture. The Bible supports one-way communication. For example, it teaches us to "be angry and yet do not sin" (Ephesians 4:26–27), "speak the truth in love" (Ephesians 4:15), "bear one another's burdens" (Galatians 6:2), and confront others (Matthew 5:23–24; 18:15–17).

Examples of One-Way Communication
Your husband will make mistakes and cause you pain. That's life with a man. To stay healthy, build respect, and keep your needs in front of his face, you must go to him and clean out your daily pain. He won't like it. That's

tough. It's good for you. It's good for him. It's good for your relationship. And because it is one-way, he'll be much better able to take in what you say and act on it.

Wife: Do you have a minute? I wanted you to know that your comment this morning about my housekeeping made me angry and offended me. I do my best, and your criticism really stung. I need praise and help with the chores, not sarcastic barbs. When you're ready, I'd appreciate hearing an apology.

Wife: I needed you last night, and you weren't there for me. I'd had a stressful day and wanted to vent to you and be comforted. You half-listened to me for five minutes, then turned the television on. I'm angry and very disappointed in you. I need you to listen to me every day.

Wife: Just give me one minute to say something. Don't respond right now; just listen. Another week has gone by, and you haven't scheduled any talk times. I'm angry with you because, even though you know this is an important need of mine, you've done nothing about it. I do not want to build up resentment against you, so I'm telling you my feelings.

Wife: It has been two weeks since you promised to schedule a meeting for us with a financial advisor. You've chosen not to do it. Hold your excuses. I don't want to hear them. I feel angry, hurt, and betrayed. If you have no intention of seeing an advisor, say so. At least that would be honest.

Wife: I have to tell you how I feel about the sex we had last night. I agreed to it, but I regret giving in to you. In the week leading up to yesterday, I was not romanced by you. I had no emotional connection to you because we hadn't talked on a deep level. I need to feel loved and close to you in order to fully participate in sex. I feel used and cheap. I'm angry because you got what you wanted and I didn't get what I needed. Sex under these circumstances is boring and a chore for me. It hurts me and pushes me away from you. If you want me to enjoy intercourse and be an active sexual partner, you have to meet my emotional and spiritual needs first.

You won't be good at this one-way communication approach for a while. No one is naturally gifted at it. It usually takes two to three months to get the hang of it. Practice. Practice. Practice. Your husband will give you many opportunities to hone your one-way skills. Keep rereading this chapter. Talk about your progress with a few members of your support team. Pray for God's help.

Remember, when practicing one-way communication, be honest, be brief, and tell your husband not to respond right away. Get in, say what you need to say, and get out. Even after a successful makeover, you'll continue to do one-way communication with him for the rest of your marriage. It will prevent him from slipping back into old habits and help him maintain the intimacy you've worked so hard to create.

Realization:
"I didn't respect you as a wife."—Ron

What went wrong?
- Ron followed the bad example of his parents' relationship.
- Nita left Ron's criticism and sarcasm unchallenged—but then gave him the silent treatment.

What's going right?
- Nita has begun asserting herself, speaking out when Ron criticizes unfairly.
- Ron is responding to his new, "strong" wife.

Next steps:
- Nita: Continue to stand up for herself.
- Ron: Treat Nita as a woman worthy of respect.

1. Are you a woman worthy of respect? If not, why not? What biblical woman do you identify with and admire most?

2. Tell your husband in what areas you don't feel respected by him. Tell him, specifically, how he can show you respect in these particular areas.

3. Do you have trouble being honest with your husband when he has hurt you in some way? What prevents you from telling him the truth?

4. Ask your husband how he thinks he'll react when you start doing one-way communication with him. Pray—right now—that God will help you both adjust to this new approach to honesty and respect.

5. Practice one-way communication right now. Tell your husband the truth about something he did or said recently. Choose something small but something that bothered you.

6. If you are being abused by your husband, immediately take the steps I described in this chapter. Tell the secret of your abuse to your support team and family. Have a meeting with them, and create a plan of action. Make sure that you will not be abused again.

Chapter 12
Marriage Makeover Achievement 9

BE AN UNDERSTANDER AND A RESPECTER

What is the greatest challenge in life for a man? Climbing Mount Everest? Winning a triathlon? Building a successful business? Becoming president of the United States?

No. No. No. And no. These challenges are easy, a piece of cake, compared to life's ultimate test for a man: living with a woman. Women are wonderful, fascinating, and exciting. Women are also difficult to please, confusing, and unpredictable—at least to men.

Picture this scene. It's a weekday morning and a man and his wife are preparing to go their separate ways. He says, "Good-bye, honey." She says, "When will you be home tonight?" The man doesn't realize it, but she has just asked a dangerous question. It's deep water.

The husband replies, "Oh, I don't know. Around 6:30." In his mind, *around* 6:30 means *around* 6:30. It's a ballpark figure. It's a range. It could be 6:40, 6:45, or even 7:00, anywhere in there. He's giving her his best guess. He's not being precise.

The woman, being a woman, zeroes in on 6:30. For her, it's not a ballpark figure. It's not a range. It's a point in time. She's thinking, "He said 6:30." So 6:30 is carved in stone in her mind. It's a guarantee. It's a promise. It's a deal. She doesn't say any of this to her husband, of course. That would be too easy. But she's thinking it.

This poor man goes off to work with no idea what he's done. He's made a deal! If he comes home at 6:40, he's late. She'll be frosty and irritated. There'll be no kiss at the front door. If he comes home at 6:45, he's really late. She'll be angry. His dinner will be put away. If he comes home at 7:00 or later, look out. He's a liar! He's broken a promise. She'll be outraged and hurt. It's going to be a long, cold night, bubba.

Sound familiar, men? Husbands, this is just one example of why we need help in dealing with women. We're out of our league! We need some kind of strategy for living with our wives in an understanding and intimate way.

I have good news for you. God has provided that strategy. Because God created your wife, He knows everything about her. He knows exactly how she needs to be treated. God, through His Word, has communicated specific guidelines on how a husband is to understand and respect his wife.

UNDERSTAND AND RESPECT HER

In 1 Peter 3:7, God, through His servant Peter, delivers a devastating message to husbands: "You husbands. . .live with your wives in an understanding way, as with someone weaker, since she is a woman; and show her honor as a fellow heir of the grace of life, so that your prayers may not be hindered."

Read that last clause again, carefully. If you don't do these actions, your prayers will be hindered. Your relationship with your heavenly Father will be limited. I'm convinced this is the reason that many husbands are spiritually dry.

You can't treat your wife poorly and be close to God. That's what the verse says. Caring for your precious wife with the understanding and respect this verse describes is obviously of paramount importance to God—so important that if you fail to do it, your communication with Him will dry up. That's the worst possible consequence.

The picture here is of handling a valuable, delicate, fragile work of art—like the *Mona Lisa*, the most famous painting in the world, which hangs in the Louvre in Paris. What if I met you at one of my marriage seminars and handed you the *Mona Lisa*? I wonder how you'd handle it.

I'll tell you how. With the most extreme care. You wouldn't want to be the guy who dropped the *Mona Lisa* and ruined it. Your wife is infinitely more valuable than a mere painting.

> *God wants you—in fact, He orders you—to handle your wife softly and gently.*

MR. INSENSITIVITY

You have some work to do in order to become a 1 Peter 3:7 kind of husband. As a man, you are most likely not a sensitive creature. In fact, it is eminently possible that you are one of the more insensitive creatures on God's green earth. You often hurt and offend your wife, and you don't even know you're doing it.

I'm not judging you, believe me. By nature, I am just as insensitive as you are. In addition to years of education, training, internship, and experience, I've had to work hard—very hard—to learn how to understand and respect Sandy and her needs. But, man, has my effort paid off! Sandy is a lot happier since I figured out how to be more sensitive. And when Sandy's happy, I'm happy.

God is also happy—and I honor Him and His Word—when I obey His 1 Peter 3:7 instructions. And when God is pleased with me, I'm happy. And, I'm able to get closer to Him.

Here are the steps I took to apply 1 Peter 3:7 to my own marriage.

Walk in Her Shoes (Pumps, Stilettos. . .)

The first step toward becoming an *understander* and a *respecter* is to walk in your wife's shoes (figuratively, guys) and realize just how insensitive you really are.

Read these words that a wife recently said to me in my therapy office—in front of her husband. (This isn't verbatim, but it's essentially accurate.)

> *I find it incredible how often my husband just doesn't get it. He walks around in his own little world, blissfully unaware of me and my needs. I know he loves me, but he can't seem to understand me. It's a real puzzle. He appears to have an IQ in the normal range. He can groom himself and get dressed without assistance. He is successful at his job. We both speak the same language. But despite these abilities, in many of our daily interactions, he completely misses what is painfully obvious to me. He just doesn't get it!*

This woman may have been a little rude, but she hit the nail on the head. I have heard this same plaintive message from thousands of wives. Your wife wants the same thing all these wives want: to be loved, to be understood, and to be respected.

It's important to your wife and your marriage that you "get it." Read the following scenarios. I've written them from the perspective of the wife. I know your wife will recognize them, and I think you will, too.

Sex Is Always the Answer. You and your husband had an argument twenty minutes ago. It did not go well. You're angry, hurt, and feel totally misunderstood. You've gone to bed early. The bedroom is dark, and you're curled up on your side of the bed. He comes into the room, crawls into bed, and snuggles up to you. You turn to him, expecting an apology and an attempt to talk through the conflict. Instead, he wants sex. The only sounds he makes are grunts. Is he some kind of animal? Yes. Does he really think that sex will solve this problem and make everything better? Yes.

Mr. Romance. Several days ago, you and your husband were talking about your upcoming wedding anniversary. You sensed that he wasn't very excited about it. He couldn't come up with any ideas for what to do. So you said that it wasn't necessary to do anything special for it. Today is the day, and sure enough, he didn't do anything special for it. To your shock, he didn't do anything at all. No card. No roses. No gift. No dinner out. He did bring home a pizza. What kind of a clueless wonder would actually think that you want nothing for your anniversary? Your husband, that's who.

The Sensitive Male. You're telling your husband about your rotten day at the office. Your male boss treated you badly in front of several coworkers. You go into detail, paying particular attention to your feelings of anger, hurt, and humiliation. Instead of helping you feel understood and comforting you, your husband responds by saying he can see your boss's point of view. He says that these things happen in offices all over the world, it's no big deal, and your boss was probably just stressed out. He looks thoughtful for a moment, and you think maybe he's realized his mistake. You ask him if he has anything else to say, and he replies, "Yeah. What's for dinner?" Your moan of anguish and frustration can be heard four houses away.

It's PMS, Isn't It? It's been a long day. Your husband forgot to call the mechanic about your car. He forgot the two items you wanted at the grocery store, but he did manage to come home with his favorite ice cream and a package of beef jerky. He commented that your chicken was a little overdone, didn't help with the dishes, and spent an hour on the computer. You've just tried to start a conversation with him, but he's focused on the television and hasn't heard a word you've said. You go into the kitchen, slam a few cupboards, and begin to cry. He comes in looking for a snack, notices you, and says, "What's wrong? Is it PMS, honey?" You want to scream, "No, it's not PMS! It's NBS, honey: No Brain Syndrome!"

It's a Man Thing

Situations like these, where the husband just doesn't get it, are not isolated occurrences. They happen all the time. You don't see what's really going on and what your wife needs from you. As my good friend John Louer likes to say, "I'm working with very small tools." Like most husbands, you have very small tools. You don't know much about relationships. You don't know your wife's basic needs, why she gets upset, or what to do to make her feel loved and secure.

The trouble is, you think you know what your wife's needs are and that you're doing a great job of meeting them. When you fail to meet your wife's needs and she gets frustrated and angry, you don't blame yourself. You blame her. Thousands of my male clients have given me the same message: "Doc, I love her. I'm doing everything I can to make her happy. I'm doing my best. I don't know why she gets all hurt and angry. It's just a woman thing. It must be hormones, being oversensitive, or just expecting too much. She's tough to please."

With their wives sitting right there in my therapy office, I've asked these same husbands to tell me the needs of their wives. All these guys have launched confidently into a list of needs. And every single husband (the whole bunch), to his shock and dismay, has been wrong. I mean, bad wrong. Not even close wrong. To a man, their mouths hang open in surprise.

Every Day, Ask What She Needs

After reading this book and doing the Makeover Steps, you will know six of your wife's basic needs and how to meet them consistently. That will greatly improve your marriage. I guarantee it.

But your wife also has important day-to-day needs that must be met. Because she is an emotional, sensitive, and periodically moody person (which are all normal traits), her daily needs can change quickly. The only way to find out what these daily needs are is to ask her at least once a day.

On the phone or in person, use words like these: "Honey, what do you need today? What can I do for you?" The first few times you ask, be prepared to catch her, because she'll faint from shock. When you jot down on your Pad what she says and follow through on meeting her needs, you'll have done your job. She'll feel understood. Respected. Loved.

When She's Upset, Ask Her to Talk

When your wife gets upset, ask her what's wrong. Tell her, in a sincere and gentle way, that you want to talk about it. If she refuses to talk about it, leave for a few minutes and then come back. Ask her again to talk to you. She needs to know you're really interested in what she has to say. She wants you to pursue her.

When she says, "I don't want to talk about it," that's not what she means. She means, "I'm not ready yet, but I want you to keep asking gently until I am ready. I'll be ready when I know you want to hear me and will handle my emotions and hurt in a tender, understanding way."

If she walks away from you before she starts talking, or during an argument, wait a few minutes, and then go after her. She may say, "Don't bother following me," and give every indication that she doesn't want you to come after her. Follow her anyway. That's what she wants.

> *She needs to know if you care enough, if you are sensitive enough, to pursue her and continue a difficult conversation.*

When she talks, whether it's about you or someone else who hurt her, *listen* and *reflect* first to build understanding. Use the communication principles I taught in chapter 8. She needs you to see what happened from her point of view.

Say "I'm Sorry"

A 1 Peter 3:7 husband says "I'm sorry" when he blows it. Many husbands can't seem to say these words. When you apologize, you have to mean it. It has to be heartfelt. It has to be repeated a number of times. You have to convince your wife that you're really sorry. Keep saying it until she feels better. Once she's been hurt, she needs your reassurance.

> *If your wife is upset and hurt, you'd better be sorry, and you'd better say it.*

Use these words in your apologies: "I'm sorry. I was wrong. I hurt you. Will you forgive me?" These phrases make it clear you "get it" and are taking responsibility for what happened. Say these words multiple times as your wife vents and talks through what happened and how it has affected her. If you pursue her, genuinely apologize multiple times, and actively listen as she talks about the incident, she will be able to feel better and forgive you.

Keep Your Voice Down

Another way to obey 1 Peter 3:7 is to lower your voice when you're angry. A loud voice and a harsh tone crush a woman. Have you ever had this happen to you? Your wife is angry and raising her voice. She's strong, she's mean. You fire back one—just one—statement in a loud voice and she dissolves into tears. Suddenly, you're the bad guy. It's because she's a very sensitive being and can't tolerate any harsh treatment. Keep your voice down. If you have an anger problem, get professional help and fix it.

Get Regular Job Evaluations
Finally, understanding and respecting your wife can be communicated by getting a job evaluation from her once a month. This takes guts, but it's what a lover does. Ask her how you're doing as her husband. Take her evaluation seriously, and make whatever adjustments are necessary. Don't assume you're doing a good job. Ask her. She's the only one who knows.

The problem:
"You became more insensitive. I noticed more irritation and anger."
—Jackie

What went wrong?
- After a few years of marriage, Brian's approach to Jackie changed from understanding to irritation.
- Brian stopped listening when Jackie disagreed or overrode her in a loud voice.
- Jackie felt like an annoyance to Brian.

What's going right?
- Brian has opened himself to change.
- Brian asks Jackie about her needs and how he can fill them.

Next steps:
- Keep talking—in a normal tone of voice.
- Meet each other's needs (the Golden Rule).

1. Husbands, which of my examples of insensitive behavior sound most familiar? Give your wife some recent examples of your insensitivity to her and to her needs. Ask her to describe the most upsetting ways you are insensitive to her.

2. Talk about insensitive male role models in your life (dad, grandpa, uncles, coaches, etc.). How did these significant men teach or model to you how to be insensitive?

3. For practice, ask your wife right now what she needs you to do for her today. Jot down these needs and follow through. (Continue to do this every day for the rest of your life.)

4. Ask your wife to evaluate your apologies—how are you doing at saying "I'm sorry"? Ask her how she'd like for you to apologize.

5. Read 1 Peter 3:7 to your wife. Pray out loud that you will, with God's help, treat her with understanding and respect. Tell God you want to obey Him, make your wife feel loved, and not be blocked from growing in your relationship with Him.

Chapter 13
Marriage Makeover Achievement 10

BE A LOVER OF SELF
(IN THE WAY GOD DESCRIBES IT)

God considers it very important for you to love yourself (Matthew 22:39). This is a love based on God's love for you and a confidence founded in Him (2 Corinthians 3:4–5). Even so, it can be very difficult to do.

There is an epidemic of poor self-esteem among American women. One reason is the nonstop cultural attack on your view of yourself. If you're not an unbelievably thin glamour queen who can juggle an amazing career and a husband and kids with ease, you're not measuring up. You're a failure.

The truth is, our culture sets up a totally false and unrealistic standard. No woman anywhere can be that good. Even the Proverbs 31 wife had her bad days.

Another, deeper, reason for poor self-esteem is unresolved pain from your past. I see many women in therapy who struggle with a negative self-image. Ninety-five percent of these women have unresolved issues with individuals in their past. Ninety-five percent! That's the bad news. The good news is that 100 percent get better when they face their pain and work through it.

Working with your husband, you need to look at the past. In fact, you'll do more than just look. You'll relive your pain, your losses, and what happened between you and others who harmed you. It's going to hurt. A lot. But it's also going to help create a healthy, God-centered love of self and a better, more intimate marriage.

DREDGE UP YOUR PAST PAIN

What I'm going to ask you to do is lay out in front of your husband—in intimate detail—all the significant pain you've experienced in your life before meeting him. You're going to write letters to every person in your past who caused you serious pain. I know you can remember at least several individuals who did or said something that you experienced as harmful. Something that tore up your heart and left a scar.

As you read these words, you are picturing in your mind's eye those individuals who traumatized you in some way in the past, aren't you? You know who they are. You haven't forgotten them or what they did to you. You may have tried to forget, but the pain is still inside you. It's time for the pain to come out.

Maybe it was your mom who hurt you. Your dad. A brother or a sister. A cousin. An uncle or an aunt. A grandparent. A stepfather or stepmother. A foster parent. A neighbor. A teacher. A coach. A Sunday school teacher or youth leader. A pastor. A boyfriend. A close female friend. A fiancé. A former spouse. A son or daughter. A boss. A fellow employee.

In addition to being angry and hurt because of what others have done to you, you probably have done things that *you* regret. Things that you're ashamed of. Things that have done damage to you and those close to you. Drinking. Drugs. Premarital sex. Lying. Gossiping. An abortion. Gambling. Overspending. An eating disorder. Divorcing someone without biblical grounds. Treating one of your children harshly. Jealousy. An explosive temper. We all have sinned. The only question is, what are your sins?

LETTERS OF TRUTH

You're going to write letters to those who have hurt you. You're also going to write letters confessing your sins and apologizing to those whom you have hurt. These letters will be the complete, honest truth in living color. You will cover all the details. You will leave nothing out. They will be heartfelt expressions of the pain you experienced.

They will be raw. Ragged. Intense. You will not spare those who hurt you or yourself from responsibility. You will not use excuses or fabricate rationalizations. You will just tell the stories and express the pain attached to the stories.

Before you write each letter, you'll pray that God will bring out the memories and the pain needed to heal.

You'll pray that God will guide you and strengthen you and comfort you. You'll pray that God will give you the ability to forgive. These letters are not to send. They are to be read only to your husband. Later you may read them to a therapist and a close friend. You may choose with God's direction and a therapist's guidance to send "cleaned up" versions of these letters to certain individuals. But for now, the letters and your pain are only for you and your husband.

I want you to write these letters even if you've already worked through your past pain with a therapist. If you didn't include your husband in the process, then you missed a step. *You* may have healed, but you overlooked a golden opportunity to change your marriage.

> *Walking through your personal journey of pain with your husband can get you inside his walls. It can lead to a break-through in communication and to an intimate connection.*

I'm asking you to do something extremely difficult. I understand that. I've led many couples through this process, and I've seen up close how emotionally demanding it is. You're going to relive the worst times in your life and allow your husband to see it and to feel it with you. This requires a lot of vulnerability. You're taking a risk, because he may not respond and open up his gates to you. But I believe it is a risk worth taking. The pain of disappointment if he chooses not to respond is outweighed by all the benefits of letting him see and feel your pain.

CHECK OUT THE BENEFITS

Here are some of the primary benefits of confronting and resolving your pain:

You'll heal from the pain. If you haven't resolved your pain, it is still inside you and it is affecting every area of your life. Now it's time for you to forgive all those who have hurt you. When you do that, you'll be healthier physically, emotionally, and spiritually. You will take a huge step toward loving yourself in the same way the Bible teaches God loves you.

You'll be a better wife because you won't transfer your pain to your husband. Your unresolved pain will be triggered, usually unintentionally, by certain words and behaviors of your husband. When that happens, your past pain will come out of you like a white-hot laser beam and hit your husband right between the eyes. Suddenly, he will not only be receiving your anger and hurt for whatever *he* did, he'll be catching it for what *others* have done to you in the past. Once you and your husband have worked through your past pain together, there will be nothing more to transfer. Your past pain won't be triggered, and you will only have to deal with your reactions to issues today, not today *and* the past.

You and your husband will be closer. Sharing your pain with your husband will bring the two of you closer in a way you have never known before. Doing this kind of deep emotional work will automatically propel your relationship to a higher level. There is an intimacy in shared pain that cannot be found in any other experience.

Your husband will learn crucial communication skills.
As you express your pain by reading letters and by sharing in follow-up conversations, your husband will learn how to listen to you, how to reflect, and how to build understanding. He'll learn, probably for the first time in his life, what it feels like to connect with someone on a deeper level. When he has reached that deeper level over and over again by helping you heal, it will be easier for him to reach that level with you in many other conversations. Once he knows how, he can do it repeatedly.

When your husband connects to your pain, he has a chance to connect to his own pain. You're not the only person with unresolved pain from the past. Your husband has plenty of his own. He has just walled himself off from it. In fact, he has walled himself off from almost all his deeper emotions. Dealing with your pain will energize his entire emotional system. When the wheels finally start turning in his emotional world, there is a pretty good chance that your past pain will trigger his past pain. Because he is getting used to feeling your pain and dealing with it, he may be able to feel his pain and share it with you.

This process, including the letters and follow-up talks, may take two or three months. Keep in mind that this is not all you'll be doing. It's just one step in the makeover. You'll still be working on the other fourteen Makeover Achievements.

Some of you reading this don't have any real traumas in your past. Your home was solid and safe, you had great parents, and your life before marriage was pretty smooth. You still need to go through this process, because it has the power to help you accept and love yourself and change your marriage. Go with the pain you do remember. No one has had a pain-free life. Dredge up whatever you can.

A WALK-THROUGH

Let me walk you through the process so you know what to do. When you've finished writing your first letter, schedule the reading for a Friday or Saturday with your husband. Give yourself enough time to read the entire letter. You'll need at least a half hour to forty-five minutes. Read the letter in the quiet, private place you use for your couple times.

Before you read the letter, take your husband's hands in yours and pray that God will direct both of you and superintend all that happens. Pray that God will help you heal and that He'll help your husband listen and understand your pain. Ideally, both of you will pray. If your husband won't pray, you go ahead and pray. After the prayer, ask your husband to do his best to reflect what you say and feel as you read the letter. Tell him it's okay to interrupt you to make statements of reflection and encouragement.

As you read the letter, pause every few paragraphs and

give your husband a chance to reflect and build understanding. When you pause, ask him to tell you what you just said and the feelings you have expressed. He needs these prompts. Since this is completely new to him, he doesn't know what he's doing. This process is one of the best ways he can learn.

Make sure you tell your husband repeatedly that you're asking for his reflection and understanding because it helps you heal. Remind him that he's working on these critical skills for *you*. To help *you*. At the same time, he's learning skills that will transform him and your marriage.

After reading the letter, thank your husband for listening and trying to feel your pain. Praise the efforts he made (Husbands need praise, remember?) Hand him a copy of the letter—do not give him a copy until after the reading—and ask him to reread it several times on his own. Ask him to pray about your pain and think about it and process it. Ask him to work hard to feel it and respond to it. Ask him to look inside himself and see what responses he has to what you've read: observations, insights, what he's learned about you, how your pain has affected you and the marriage, his own emotions, events and pain in his life that your letter triggered, and so on.

It's a good idea to pray together again at the end of the letter reading. In your prayer, thank God for a husband who is willing to go through this process with you. Ask God to help your husband process your pain and respond to it. Finally, schedule the follow-up meetings.

You need to have at least two follow-ups a week so you keep the pain fresh and your husband engaged. Leave a few days between meetings to allow sufficient time for each of you to process. I recommend Monday and Thursday for these meetings. They should be fifteen to twenty minutes long. If they are any longer, your husband will get distracted and overwhelmed. Sometimes, if you're both getting into it and he's okay with continuing, you may want to go longer. How many follow-ups will you have? At least six, and maybe even eight. You need this many to vent and process and heal. Your husband needs this many to practice emotionally connecting to you.

In these follow-up meetings, begin again with prayer. Briefly ask God to be with you as you work together. Choose a quiet, private place—ideally, the same spot you use to read the letters. Screen out all distractions.

After the prayer, ask your husband if he has any responses to share. These responses could be to the letter or to other follow-up meetings you've had. If he shares something, great. Reflect what he says, and interact with him about it. If he has nothing to say, which may be the case early in the process, move right into verbally processing the letter. Vent your feelings and thoughts and pain. Tell him the additional details and memories and insights that God has brought up in the past few days.

As you express yourself in these follow-up meetings, pause occasionally—just as you did when you read the letter—and ask your husband to reflect and try to understand your pain. Give him the words and phrases to use, because he won't know what to say.

At the close of each follow-up, pray again. Pray that God will continue to help each of you process the pain. Thank your husband for spending the time and trying to help you in the healing process. Ask him to pray and process between now and the next follow-up.

Near the end of each cycle of letter and follow-ups, around the sixth or seventh follow-up meeting, ask your husband to write a letter to you containing his summary of the process. Ask him to put on paper what you've shared verbally, your feelings, and his responses to your pain. Tell him to do his best and not to worry about being right or wrong. Tell him you just want to hear from his heart. Ask him to do it for you. Make it clear that hearing him read this kind of letter will promote your healing. If he'll do it, it will also help him reach a deeper level in his own emotional life and in his relationship with you. Something about writing down pain and feelings and emotional responses is healthy and healing.

Follow this same procedure until you have expressed all the significant pain from your past: Write a letter; read it out loud to your husband; take time to process; conduct your series of follow-up meetings; and have your husband write a summary letter. Be prepared for this process to be very difficult for both you and your husband. It will require faith in God and perseverance. It will hurt in many ways. But it has the potential to make a huge, positive impact on you, your husband, and your relationship. It has the potential to give your husband a taste of the emotional intimacy he has been missing his whole life. It has the potential to give you the emotional intimacy you both have been missing in your marriage.

THE HUSBAND'S TURN

Once you have processed all of your pain, it's a good idea for your husband to follow these same steps. He has his own pain from the past that needs to be expressed. He can experience all the benefits from doing what you've done.

So I recommend that you—as a couple—reverse the process and allow the husband to write the letters and work through his own pain. Go ahead and ask him to do it. Since you've gone first and he has helped you get through it, he should be more inclined to take his turn.

Realization:
"I never understood why my beautiful, intelligent, and talented wife didn't like herself."—John

What went wrong?
- Long-standing self-esteem issues have held Becky back.
- John has tried, unsuccessfully, to help Becky accept herself.

What's going right?
- The letter-writing exercise uncovered Becky's issues from her childhood and first marriage.
- Knowing the issues helps Becky and John deal with the problems.

Next steps:
- Work through John's past hurts with a letter-writing process.

1. Tell your husband what you think of yourself. What is your self-esteem like? Do you love yourself in a healthy, God-directed and God-centered way? What do you think are your strengths and weaknesses?

2. Ask your husband to tell you what he thinks of you. What does he believe to be your strengths and weaknesses? What does God think of you? If God views you this way, what should your self-image be?

3. If a healthy, biblical self-image has been lacking, how has this negatively affected your life?

4. Tell your husband who has significantly hurt you in the past. Give names and details of what happened.

5. Commit, together, to follow the strategy of letters and follow-up talks. Tell your husband now the name of the person to whom you will write your first letter. Pray that God will guide you, as a couple, through this painful process.

6. Husbands, are you willing to follow this strategy and deal with your past pain after your wife has done her work? What obstacles would prevent you from saying yes?

Chapter 14
Marriage Makeover Achievement 11

BE A ROMANCER

For a woman, there is no real love without romance. I have not seen a single exception to this rule in my twenty-plus years as a clinical psychologist and seminar leader. Not one. Your wife needs to be romanced regularly by you. If you fail to be a romancer, she will feel unloved and have an ache in her heart that will not go away.

Most men are romantic only during courtship. We're not stupid. We realize what it takes to get a woman to say yes to a marriage proposal. When we're pursuing a woman, we're as romantic as can be. Wining and dining and flowering and candying and talking. Yes, even talking! We're not going to talk after marriage, but she doesn't have to know that.

When we've bagged our woman—like every great hunter—we put her up on the wall in the den and find new fields to conquer. The pressure is off. Mission accomplished. We were Sir Lancelot, her dashing romantic hero on the white horse. Now we're Archie Bunker, her boring stick wearing a hole in the recliner.

Listen, men. When you stop the romance, your woman assumes you don't love her anymore. And she's absolutely right—from her perspective, and that's what we're talking about. You can't convince her otherwise because she must be romanced to feel loved.

You say, "I'm just not a romantic guy." I say, "Fine. *Get over it.* Your wife needs romance!"

GOD LOVES ROMANCE

The observation that your wife needs to be romanced didn't originate with me. It's not my idea. It's God's idea. God created woman, and He makes it clear that she needs her husband to romance her. God loves romance, and He wants it to be an integral part of every marriage. There's one whole book in the Bible devoted to romance, love, and sex—the Song of Solomon.

You've heard of the *Reader's Digest* condensed versions of popular books? Well, here is the Dave Clarke condensed version of the Song of Solomon:

Boy meets girl.
Boy and girl fall in love.
Boy is very romantic as he courts girl.
Boy and girl get married.
Boy continues to romance girl for the rest of their married life.

Girl is happy, boy is happy, their marriage is terrific. God is pleased and blesses them.

The boy is King Solomon. The girl is a Shulammite woman. The Song of Solomon is the story of their courtship and marriage. The joy, passion, and fulfillment they experienced leaps off the pages of this book. God wants their story to be your story. And it can be if you romance your wife. That's what the Song of Solomon is all about. That's the secret to the powerful and enduring love between Solomon and his Shulammite wife.

THE POWER OF VERBAL ROMANCE

Read Song of Solomon 2:8–9, and you'll get a clear picture of how the Shulammite felt about her man, Solomon:

"Listen! My beloved!
Behold, he is coming,
Climbing on the mountains,
Leaping on the hills!
My beloved is like a gazelle or a young stag.
Behold, he is standing behind our wall,
He is looking through the windows,
He is peering through the lattice."

The Shulammite is at home, and Solomon has been out doing whatever kings do. Solomon is now coming back home, and these verses describe the Shulammite's anticipation of his return. As he gets closer and closer, she is so excited she can barely contain herself. She even calls him a "young stag." When was the last time your wife called you a young stag? Yeah. I thought so.

Does your wife look forward to your coming home like this? Does she tremble with excitement when she hears your car in the driveway? Does her heart flutter with passion as she rushes up to greet you? Probably not. You're lucky if she says, "Hi, honey," and gives you a token kiss on the cheek.

Why can't the Shulammite wait to see her man? Why does she go into spasms of joy when she knows he's about to come in the door? The answer is found in the Song of Solomon 4:1–5. Here are some excerpts from these verses:

> *"How beautiful you are, my darling,*
> *How beautiful you are!*
> *Your eyes are like doves behind your veil;*
> *Your hair is like a flock of goats*
> *That have descended from Mount Gilead.*
> *Your teeth are like a flock of newly shorn ewes. . . .*
> *Your lips are like a scarlet thread,*
> *And your mouth is lovely.*
> *Your temples are like a slice of a pomegranate. . . .*
> *Your neck is like the tower of David. . . .*
> *Your two breasts are like two fawns."*

Do you get it? Solomon romanced his lady. He treated her like a queen. He showered her with romantic pictures of how gorgeous she was. That's why she loved him so much and looked forward to seeing him. She couldn't wait to return his love.

If you want your woman to respond with the Shulammite's passion and intensity, you need to verbally romance her. Tell her often how beautiful she is. Now, some cultural context is needed here. Please don't try Solomon's descriptions today. A husband called me after he and his wife attended one of my marriage seminars. He said, "Dave, your Song of Solomon romantic idea didn't work for me."

"What do you mean?" I asked.

"The other day, my wife and I were coming out of church. I told her that the sunlight made her hair look like a flock of goats. She was insulted."

I said, "You dummy! Those lines in chapter 4 of the Song of Solomon worked only back in those days. You need to come up with contemporary romantic descriptions." You just can't help some people.

Solomon verbalized his love on a regular basis. He did it all the time. He went overboard. Not just, "Love ya, honey." Solomon is our example.

> You say, "I'm just not an expressive guy." I say, "Fine. Get over it! Your wife, just like the Shulammite, needs to hear how beautiful she is, over and over and over."

Your wife is the most beautiful woman in the world. Right? Well then, tell her. Compliment her physical beauty. Her emotional beauty. Her spiritual beauty. Do it out loud, right to her face. Do it often. A woman never gets tired of this. The Shulammite never said, "Oh, Solomon, stop! You're embarrassing me with all these compliments." She just drank in his verbal romance. It filled her heart with love, and she loved him right back.

I'm not asking you to be like Solomon twenty-four hours a day. Frankly, no one has that kind of stamina. Just romance your wife regularly and see what happens. She'll feel loved! And that's your job: to be sure that she feels loved.

You'll be loved in return. You want your wife to be warm, soft, and attentive to your needs, don't you? Wouldn't you like her to be more interested in sex and more responsive in the bedroom? Of course! That's what all husbands want. Then romance her. It will be returned to you a hundred times over.

CREATE A LITTLE ROMANCE

To help get you started, here are some behaviors that your wife *and* you will find romantic:

One Date a Week

I strongly recommend that you take your wife out on a date once a week. Just the two of you. No children. That's what babysitters are for. In fact, you be the one to call the babysitter and sign her up. Make sure you have a list of three or four teenage girls. Once they get a social life (i.e., a boyfriend), it's the kiss of death. If you can get a family member to stay with your kids for free, fine. Or maybe you can babysit another couple's kids one night and they can babysit yours the next night.

Early in the week, look into your wife's lovely eyes and ask her, "Would you like to go out with me this Saturday night?" I say Saturday because that's my date night with Sandy. Women like to be asked. Sandy and I go out every Saturday night, but I still ask her every Monday or Tuesday. She doesn't say, "Why are you asking me? I know we're going out Saturday. We always do." Oh, no. My queen smiles and says, "Yes, Dave. I'd love to go out Saturday."

Don't make your wife always come up with what you're going to do. You have a brain, don't you? At least every other week, you decide the plan for the date. Be creative. Plan something you think she'd enjoy.

A Walk in the Evening

Taking a walk together around your neighborhood in the evening can be very romantic. Do this two or three times a week. It's low-key, relaxing, and fun. Just make sure you hold her hand. The physical contact is what creates the romantic mood. You're not walking with your mother, your aunt, or your sister. You're walking with your sweetheart! So hold her hand.

I've had husbands whine to me, "Oh, but it's too hot to walk!" I tell these babies, "I know it's hot. That's the beauty of it. Walk with her, get all sweaty, then take a shower together. It's not about the walk; it's about the shower."

A Small Gift

About once a month, buy your wife an inexpensive little something. She will absolutely love the fact that you thought about her. It's not the gift, but the love and thoughtfulness behind it that she'll appreciate. Don't give the gift to her in a plain old store bag. This isn't dog food or groceries. Have someone at the store wrap it, or wrap it yourself.

A Romantic Card

Once every two weeks, give your dear wife a greeting card with a romantic message. This card must be gushy, mushy, and sentimental. Not, "Be My Friend," but, "Your Stunning Beauty and Sweet Spirit Bring Color and Life into My Dark and Lonely World," or "You Are My Perfect Mate; You Satisfy the Deepest Longings of My Heart." You get the idea.

Please, please, please, don't just sign your name in the card. Your wife wants to read a paragraph from you about how much you love her and why. You don't have to be Shakespeare. No one's going to publish your little love notes. Compliment her. Thank her for being who she is. Write from your heart. She'll love you for doing it.

Ask Her What She Finds Romantic

Most wives will feel loved if you try to create some romance. But these loving gestures are just the tip of the romantic iceberg. Your wife needs to be romanced in a variety of ways. To make sure you're being her Sir Lancelot, ask her once every two months what she finds romantic. She thinks about romance all the time. She gets ideas about romance from her friends, books and magazines, and her own imagination. So she'll have a little list of romantic ideas every time you ask. Write the ideas down on your Pad, follow through and do them, and you'll be her romantic hero.

Touching without Intercourse

Read that heading again: "Touching without Intercourse." Do you have any idea what this is? Like most men, I didn't used to know. After years of research, I have made a stunning discovery. I may win the Nobel Prize in Science for my breakthrough. I hope you're sitting down. Here it is: It is possible to touch a female *without* moving on to intercourse.

Now, I've only tested this on laboratory rats. But they're doing quite well. I just know you human husbands can do it.

Touch your wife. Kiss her. Rub her neck. Make out with her and. . .that's all. *Don't ask for intercourse.* Can you picture this? She'll be shocked. She'll say, "Honey, don't you want something else?" You'll say, "No, sweetheart, I'm just loving you for you." You won't mean it, but you'll say it. And you'll stick to it. Do this almost every day.

Obviously, there are times when you do move on to intercourse. God wants intercourse to be a regular part of every married couple's life together. But not every time you touch her. If every time you lay a hand on your wife, you push for intercourse, she'll feel used and cheap. Ask your wife if that's true. She'll tell you that Dr. Clarke is, once again, correct. Of course I'm correct. I'm an expert. (Actually, I've learned this truth the hard way from my wife.)

If, however, she insists on intercourse and begs you for it, go ahead. If that's a need she has, it's your sworn duty as her husband to meet it. As you frequently romance your queen and regularly touch her without expecting intercourse, there may actually be times when she says to you, "Young stag, take me! Take me now!"

Romance Her When You Don't Have To

Don't romance your wife only on special occasions like her birthday, Valentine's Day, and your anniversary. Lots of dimwit husbands in the world do that! God help you if you fail to come through on these dates. Romance her for no reason other than because you love her. That's what it's all about. You don't do it because you have to. You don't do it because she expects you to. You do it because you love her, and you want her to know that and feel that.

Whatever you do, don't start romance and then stop.

This crushes a woman. It's better not to start at all than to start and then stop. All you have to do is keep up a steady stream of romance until you're dead. When you're dead, I'll let you off the hook. Your last words in the hospital, as you squeeze your wife's hand, ought to be, "Well, I guess we're not going out on our date this weekend." And then, you're gone. And your legacy is that of a man who loved his woman and romanced her to the end.

SNAPSHOT
ASHLEY AND GREG

Realization:
"About two years into our marriage, all the romance was gone."—Ashley

What went wrong?
- Greg's romantic initiatives during dating disappeared shortly into the marriage.
- Ashley didn't feel loved or attractive.
- Sex became a chore rather than a passionate pleasure.

What's going right?
- Greg has begun initiating romance again—cards, flowers, and other gifts.
- Ashley is responding favorably—even in the bedroom.

Next steps:
- Greg: Continue the small, but very important, efforts at romance.
- Ashley: Continue to respond.

1. Husband, how are you as a romancer? On a scale from one to ten (one being the most unromantic guy who ever lived, and ten being Sir Lancelot, Casanova, and Cary Grant rolled into one amazing romantic hero), rate yourself. What have you done in the past week that would be classified by your wife as romantic? How about the past two weeks?

2. Ask your wife to rate you as a Romancer. Take her assessment like a man, and believe it.

3. If you need to improve in this area, what keeps you from romancing your wife? What romantic behaviors did you do in the past when you were dating her?

4. Ask your wife which of my suggested romantic behaviors she would like you to do on a regular basis. Ask her to brainstorm with you and list behaviors she would find romantic.

5. Ask her on a date (for this week) right now. Get the babysitter scheduled if you have children, and plan the date yourself.

6. Take your queen's hand, and pray that, with God's help, you will be a romancer for the rest of your lives.

Chapter 15
Marriage Makeover Achievement 12

BE A PRAISER

If you want to know the way to your husband's heart, read the Song of Solomon. If you want to learn how to motivate your husband to meet your deepest needs, read the Song of Solomon. If you want to be the wife God wants you to be, read the Song of Solomon.

Solomon was the happiest husband in the world. He was thrilled. He was deeply satisfied. He felt confident, safe, and secure. His book is called the *Song* of Solomon because he was whistling a happy tune. Why was he so joyful? Two words: Shulammite woman.

Solomon's Shulammite wife was an amazing woman. She knew exactly what she was doing as a wife. She made it her business to meet Solomon's needs. She was attentive, affectionate, and incredibly complimentary. Solomon was her hero. That's what your husband needs to be—your hero!

The Shulammite woman knew the secret to loving a man and connecting with him on the most intimate level possible: she *respected* him. She realized that one of a husband's most important needs is to be respected by his wife. She respected Solomon on every page of the book. She respected him every day of their life together. She lifted him up. She constantly praised his worth. She honored him for who he was and what he did. She made him feel like a real man.

What was the result of the Shulammite's respect for Solomon? What did he do in return? He loved her with a love so passionate and sensitive and tender that it boggles the mind. I mean, when you're reading the Song of Solomon, you just can't quite believe how loving Solomon was. You think, *Oh, please, he couldn't have been that fantastic of a husband.* But he was. That's what the Bible says.

Solomon was affectionate. He was focused on the Shulammite's needs. He showered her with words and actions that expressed his love. He treated her like a queen. Best of all, he opened up and talked to her. And not just about the weather or the rusty wheels on his chariot. He shared personal, intimate things about himself, about her, and about their relationship. He gave himself to her.

Solomon did everything every wife wants her husband to do. What motivated him to be this kind of husband was the respect the Shulammite gave him. That was her secret to getting the marriage partner of her dreams. You can do the same thing she did. I'm going to show you how.

PETER, PAUL, AND MARRIAGE

If the example of the Shulammite isn't enough to convince you of the importance of respecting your husband, read the marital teachings of Peter and Paul. Both of these giants of the early church highlight the husband's need to be respected by his wife.

Peter makes the point that husbands can be changed by their wives, even come to faith in Christ, "as they observe your chaste and respectful behavior" (1 Peter 3:2). Just a few verses later, in 1 Peter 3:6, he expands his instruction on respect: "Sarah obeyed Abraham, calling him lord, and you have become her children if you do what is right without being frightened by any fear."

In case you were wondering, you don't have to call your husband "lord." He'd probably love it, but that's going a little too far. But God does want you to give your husband the kind of respect that Sarah gave Abraham. She recognized him as the leader of their marriage and family.

Paul concludes his powerful section on marriage in Ephesians 5 with this final charge for husbands and wives: "Each individual among you also is to love his own wife even as himself; and the wife must see to it that she respects her husband" (v. 33). As Paul drives home so clearly in that last line, there is nothing more important a wife can do than respect her husband. You must treat him as someone who is important and worthy. Someone whom you admire and who is impressive to you.

God commands you to respect your husband. It's not an option. And when your husband feels respected by you, he's much more likely to make the changes you want him to make.

How do you respect your husband? You do the big *P*.

PRAISE HIM

Men thrive on praise. It is our lifeblood. It is what gives us energy, confidence, power, and passion. Have you ever seen your husband and a group of his male friends watching a football or basketball game together? Or playing a sport? There's a lot of praise and encouragement flying around, isn't there? "Way to go"; "Atta boy"; "Great shot"; "That was sweet"; and other expressions of positive reinforcement are given freely and often. The guys are always back-slapping, knuckle-butting, and high-fiving each other.

Your husband needs approval and encouragement, and he needs it from you. If Sandy doesn't praise me on a regular basis, I don't feel loved by her. She can be doing all kinds of things for me, but without her praise, I feel insecure and discouraged. I think she's not impressed with me and what I'm doing at work and in the home. I get quieter and I withdraw from her. Sound familiar?

If you want to deflate your husband's ego and drive

him away from you, just continue not to praise him. I say "continue" because I'll bet you're not very good at praising him. You tend to notice all the things he doesn't do, don't you? And you point those mistakes out to him, don't you? And you overlook the positive things he does do for you and the family, don't you?

> *Your husband needs praise just as you need personal talk and emotional connection.*

If you think you're praising your husband enough, you'd better make sure. Ask him how you're doing in the praise department. Whatever he says, concentrate on praising him as much as you can. You can't praise too much. You do have to be honest with him about his mistakes, but at the same time, you'd better be praising him for what he's doing right.

Compliment your husband often. Use the Shulammite woman as your example. The Shulammite was very flattering to Solomon. I mean, it's almost sickening to read the many sweet things she showered on him. Read this description she gives of Solomon: "My beloved is like a gazelle or a young stag" (Song of Solomon 2:9).

Young Stag was evidently one of the Shulammite's favorite pet names for Solomon. She uses it again in 2:17 and 8:14. In today's language, stag means *stud*. Once or twice a week, when your husband comes home from work say, "How are you, stud?" He is a stud! He's the only stud you've got. I guarantee you, he'll like it.

Tell your husband he's handsome. He's charming. He's outstanding as a worker and as a family man. Comment positively on his character and integrity. Tell him he looks sharp in his blue blazer and khaki pants. Mention that he's one of the few men you know who makes a real effort to keep his nose hairs clipped. Whatever. You get the idea. Just compliment him on a regular basis.

Thank him for working at his job. Nobody thanks him for doing that job. He needs you to thank him at least once a week. Thank him for the jobs—no matter how few—he does around the house. Thank him for behavior you like. The next time he takes out the trash, run down the driveway and high-five him: "Give me five, baby! Way to go with that trash!" Then slap him on the bottom and say in a loud voice so the neighbors can hear, "You are my trash man!"

The next time he unloads the dishwasher, *it's a big honking deal!* Say something nice and positive to him. You'll be thinking: *Big whoop! I've unloaded that thing the last eight hundred ninety-nine times. He'll probably put the dishes away in the wrong spots anyway.* Don't say it! Say: "Thank you, young stag. That's an outstanding job! You are the dishwasher unloading man!"

Have you noticed your husband fishing for compliments and praise? He'll do some small job and mention it to you: "Hey, I put gas in your car." "I did a load of laundry for you." "I took out that big, smelly garbage bag." If he's fishing, you're not doing your job. Don't make him beg for your praise; give it to him all the time.

If you don't praise him, he'll assume you don't care about the job he did. He'll assume you don't care about him. He'll assume he can't ever please you. He'll assume you don't love him. If you praise him regularly, you'll kill three birds with one stone. He'll continue the behavior you praised and do even more, hoping for more praise. He'll also feel loved. The third—and best—bird is that your praise will help motivate him to become a better husband. Your praise gives him confidence and security. Your praise makes him feel closer to you. Your praise will give you more influence in his life, motivating him to try to please you in the areas most important to you: spirituality, communication, needs, romance, and leadership. So start praising your husband and never stop.

CONNECT THE DOTS

Your husband won't automatically see the connection between his loving behavior and your loving behavior in response. And he needs to see that connection, because it will motivate him to keep on doing the behaviors you need. So don't just praise his behavior and drop it. Praise what he does, and then tell him specifically how his positive behavior has produced a loving response from you.

Tell your husband in detail that because he loved you in a specific way, shared something personal, did a romantic behavior, prayed with you, or met another one of your needs— you did something loving for him in return.

Connect the dots for him every single time: "When you did A for me, I did B for you."

Wife: I put in extra work on this meal because you did those three nasty chores for me yesterday. (Don't kid yourself; one of the ways to a man's heart *is* through his stomach.)

Wife: Do you want to know why I asked you for sex and was more responsive just now in bed? It's not just because you have the body of a Greek god. It's because you initiated that talk time last night and spent twenty minutes in conversation with me. (Message: more talk equals more and better sex.)

Wife: I'm rubbing your feet now because two hours ago you listened to my long story about the conflict with my girlfriend. I needed to vent, and you were there.

Wife: Do you know why I just sat through that action-adventure movie with you? It's not because I like to see bombs going off, people screaming in terror, and dead bodies flying around. I did it because three days ago you sat with me and watched that chick flick on television.

Wife: When you prayed with me just now, I felt so loved by you. And I love and respect you more. When we pray together, I see you as my leader and my hero. It makes me want to do all kinds of loving things for you. (Do several loving behaviors in the next few days and tell him it's because he prayed with you.)

I know what you're thinking: *Why do I have to praise him every time? Shouldn't he do these behaviors just because they're the right things to do and because God commands him to do them?* Yes, he should do the loving husband behaviors for these reasons and not because you're praising him. But, the fact is, your connect-the-dots praise will be a huge motivating factor in his doing what you need him to do. So don't quibble and get stuck in technicalities. Go ahead and praise him in this strategic way, and it will be well worth your effort. Remember, praising your husband is a biblical principle.

SNAPSHOT
ROB AND MEG

Realization:
"I always wanted and needed your respect."
—Rob

What went wrong?
- Rob felt that Meg viewed him as "every other guy in the world—nothing special."
- Rob felt that Meg wasn't interested in his work.
- Meg criticized Rob's help around the house, causing him to withdraw further.

What's going right?
- Meg is making a concerted effort to praise Rob.
- Rob is responding favorably—wanting to do more around the house and to spend time with Meg.

Next steps:
- Meg: Continue to praise Rob.
- Rob: Stay "plugged in" at home.

1. How are you doing in the area of praising your husband? On a scale from one to ten (one being little or no praise, and ten being regular and frequent praise like the Shulammite), rate yourself as a praiser. Ask your husband to rate you.

2. If you haven't been a good praiser, why do you think that is? What in your childhood, previous relationships, personality, and/or current marriage is stopping you from praising your husband?

3. Name some behaviors your husband does regularly for which you can praise him. Right now, praise him for three behaviors he has done this week and three things about him—his personality, his character— that you appreciate.

4. Ask your husband what behaviors he does (or will begin to do) for which he wants your praise.

5. Pray together now, and tell God you will, with His help, work hard to regularly recognize your husband's qualities and efforts and praise him.

Chapter 16
Marriage Makeover Achievement 13

BE A LEADER

Quite a bit of confusion exists in the world today about leadership in the marriage and the home. But God is not confused. Here is God's decision on the subject: "Wives, be subject to your own husbands, as to the Lord. For the husband is the head of the wife, as Christ also is the head of the church, He Himself being the Savior of the body. But as the church is subject to Christ, so also the wives ought to be to their husbands in everything" (Ephesians 5:22–24).

That's a pretty clear message, isn't it? Headship equals leadership. As husbands, we have been given by God the job of leader: in the marriage relationship and in the home.

More husbands fail in this area than in almost any other. Why? Because being a leader is very difficult. How do we figure out the right way to lead our wives? By looking to Jesus. As in every area of life, we need to follow the example Jesus Christ set when He walked the earth.

LEAD AS CHRIST LED

To be a biblical leader, we must lead as Christ led. In Matthew 20:28, Jesus summed up His leadership style: "The Son of Man did not come to be served, but to serve, and to give His life a ransom for many."

One of the most powerful illustrations of Christ's commitment to lead by serving is found in John 13:3–5. Read the following verses and try to picture in your mind what Jesus is doing.

> *Jesus, knowing that the Father had given all things into His hands, and that He had come forth from God and was going back to God, got up from supper, and laid aside His garments; and taking a towel, He girded Himself. Then He poured water into the basin, and began to wash the disciples' feet and to wipe them with the towel with which He was girded.*

Can you imagine this scene? Jesus Christ is washing the disciples' dirty, dust-covered feet! This is the King of the universe washing feet! Why? Because that's what a leader does.

> The bottom line is this: Christ, God and Savior, is a servant-leader, one who leads by identifying the needs of others and meeting them. Husbands are to be servant-leaders, leading their wives by serving them.

If you lead by serving, your wife will follow you anywhere. If you serve your wife faithfully by meeting her needs, you make it easier for her to submit to you. You make it easier for her to support you in a decision with which she disagrees. You make it easier for her to love and respect you. You make it easier for her to meet your needs.

Here are four practical ways you can be a servant-leader:

1. Do Your Share of the Household Chores

Don't just do the bare minimum of chores. Do *more* than you have to do. This is the most obvious way to be a servant-leader. Can you see Jesus living in a home and not being helpful? Sitting on the couch? Avoiding jobs? No way!

I know you're thinking about what's best for your wife when you don't do much around the house: You're trying to prepare her for widowhood. Of course, I'm joking. You're just being selfish and lazy. I know, because that's how I used to be.

My Sandy wants to be on a team, and your wife wants to be on a team. The house is extremely important to a woman, and she needs your help to keep it in good condition. Ask your wife every day what chores need to be done. Do your jobs faithfully *and* ask her for extra jobs. She'll feel closer to you. She'll follow you. She'll have more time and energy for you.

2. Meet Her Needs

If you're not meeting your wife's needs, you're not doing

your job as a servant-leader. You don't meet all her needs; just the needs a husband can meet. Unlike Jesus, you don't know what her needs are. Don't assume you know. You'll be wrong. The *only* way to find out is to ask her every day—more than once—what her needs are. Your wife is an emotional, unpredictable creature, and so her needs will change throughout the day. Ask her in the morning before you go to work. Call her at lunchtime and ask her. When you get home from work, ask her again.

Make it clear to her that you're not just willing to do chores. You're asking her to tell you her physical, emotional, and spiritual needs. The whole enchilada. And, you'll do your best to meet them. Just asking communicates love and concern. Following through is even better. Do what I do when I ask Sandy her needs. To make certain I don't forget, I jot them down on my Pad. I don't want to disappoint her.

3. Always Include Her in Decisions

Always, always, always ask your wife for input before making a significant decision. Consider your wife's viewpoint, her wisdom, and her intuition. She's your equal partner in the relationship, so treat her as an equal. Besides, how can you expect her to support you in a decision she had no part in making?

> *It's demeaning, insulting, and a failure in servant-leadership to make decisions without consulting your wife.*

Involve your wife in the finances. She needs to know where every penny is. Make financial decisions together. Major purchases, the development of a budget, investments, and tithing all require her input. I know husbands who tell their wives nothing about the money. Why? Is it a secret? Are you in the CIA? Tell her! Keep her involved.

4. Be Her Champion

Your woman is more than a wife and a mother. She is a person—with her own gifts, abilities, hopes, and dreams. Every wife needs to develop her own life *outside the home*. She needs her own identity, her own activities, and her own unique way of affecting the world for Christ. She loves being a wife and mom, but she needs more.

One of your jobs as a servant-leader is to be her champion as she branches out and fulfills her dreams as an independent person. Ask her what she wants to do with other facets of her life. It may be time with her friends, more education, a job outside the home, service in the church, a hobby, or a combination of all these. When she tells you what she needs, do everything you can to help her. She's done a lot for you and the kids, hasn't she? Now, it's her turn to fly.

She won't go crazy and leave you and the kids in the

lurch. She won't run off to Hawaii to follow her dream of surfing the Banzai Pipeline. She'll still be a great wife and mom. What will happen is that she'll be joyful, content, confident, and energized as a person. And she'll be appreciative of the man who encouraged and helped her spread her wings.

LEAD YOUR WIFE SPIRITUALLY

Part of being a godly man is leading your wife spiritually. Take a look at Ephesians 5:24 again: "But as the church is subject to Christ, so also the wives ought to be to their husbands in everything." The husband is to lead in *everything*. Everything means everything, including the spiritual area. Ephesians 5:25–31 describes a husband who leads by caring for his wife in a compassionate, tender, and attentive way. Your job as a loving leader is to make sure that every facet of your precious wife's life is healthy. Her spiritual life is, in fact, the most important part of who she is.

> *Your wife's deepest individual need, from a biblical perspective, is for you to help her maintain a close, growing relationship with Jesus Christ.*

How can you lead your wife spiritually? By scheduling regular times of prayer and spiritual sharing with your wife. Is this tough? Man, is it ever! This is one of the hardest things I do as a husband. I often feel uncomfortable, threatened, awkward, and incompetent. Even after four years of working on a spiritual bond with Sandy, I find that Satan tries to block me every step of the way. He knows that these spiritual bonding behaviors are essential to a healthy marriage. He knows that he can't destroy our marriage if we're regularly praying together and talking about our spiritual lives.

Is it worth it? Oh, yeah, it sure is. Sandy and I are stronger and closer than we have ever been. Joining spiritually, for just a few minutes a week, has revived our passion and intimacy. It's still hard to lead Sandy spiritually, but I'm going to keep on doing it. It's what God wants me to do. It's what Sandy needs me to do. It's what is keeping our marriage alive and well.

I want you to do two things. First, sit down with your wife every Saturday or Sunday evening and schedule three five-minute prayer sessions for the upcoming week. If you don't schedule them, you won't do them. So schedule them. These can be part of your twenty- to thirty-minute couple times. When the appointed time comes, go to your wife and ask her to pray with you. Sit down in a quiet, private place in your home, just the two of you, and list prayer requests. Then hold hands and pray one at a time.

At first, you'll pray for safe topics: your children, your family, health concerns, your church, and people you know. As you go along, you'll start sharing and praying for more personal, intimate issues: your worries, your fears, your dreams, spiritual weaknesses, God's guidance in your life, and protection against Satan's attacks.

The second thing, which you'll schedule at the same time as your prayer sessions, is to meet with your wife at the end of every week for a spiritual evaluation. Because life is so busy, this is a great way to stay spiritually connected as a couple. For a total of fifteen or twenty minutes, both you and your wife share what happened in your spiritual lives in the past week. What you learned in your daily quiet times with God. How you applied the Bible. What God taught you. Spiritual victories. Spiritual defeats. (If you want to learn more about how to spiritually bond as a husband and wife, read my book *A Marriage after God's Own Heart.*)

These two spiritual activities will get you headed in the right direction. Don't think you have to be a spiritual giant to do this. Don't think you really have to know what you're doing. Just do it. You won't be alone. God will help you. Your wife will be patient and kind. She'll work with you as you bond spiritually.

Men, don't be a leader just for your wife. It is very good for her, that's true. But that's not the real point. Do it for God. *He* wants you to grow spiritually and to lead your wife in a spiritual bond.

SNAPSHOT
DEBBIE AND TOM

The problem:
"I never thought you'd be the leader in our home."—Debbie

What went wrong?
- Debbie viewed Tom as weak and took over leadership duties.
- Debbie resisted Tom when he stepped up to lead.

What's going right?
- Debbie acknowledged Tom's biblical role as family leader.
- Tom welcomes Debbie's input on decisions.
- Debbie feels less stressed without leadership duties.

Next steps:
- Keep talking and praying together.
- Tom: Lead.
- Debbie: Support.

1. Did anyone in your childhood and young adulthood teach you to lead your wife and family? What kind of leader was your dad?

2. What makes it so tough to be the leader in your marriage and home? What prevents you from leading?

3. Evaluate yourself in the four areas of servant-leadership described in this chapter: doing your share of the household chores, meeting your wife's needs, always including her in decisions, and being her champion. Ask your wife to gently but honestly evaluate you in these areas.

4. Ask your wife what specific actions she wants you to do as her leader. Tell her what she can do to help you lead in these ways.

5. Right now, schedule three five-minute prayer sessions with your wife for the coming week. If you want to, you can pray at the beginning or end of three of your thirty-minute couple times.

6. Right now, schedule your first weekly spiritual evaluation meeting.

Chapter 17
Marriage Makeover Achievement 14

BE PLAYFUL, AND PURSUE HIM SEXUALLY

Your husband needs your time and attention. He probably won't tell you this, but it's true. If he thinks he's way down on your list of priorities, he'll be angry and resentful and hurt. And, it's your fault. You're not doing your job as his wife. Take a good look at your life. What is ahead of your husband on your list of priorities? Your children? Your family? Your service in the church? Your job outside the home? Your housework? Your friends? Your Bible study group? Many wives have a bad habit of putting these people and activities before their husbands.

> By nature, wives will take care of all their jobs and responsibilities first; then, if they have any time and energy left, they will tend to their husbands. This is backward according to the Bible.

Your relationship with God comes first, but God wants your husband to be your number two priority in life. Don't put him last or even third.

In Titus 2:4–5, Paul instructs the older women in the church to "encourage the young women to love their husbands, to love their children, to be sensible, pure, workers at home, kind, being subject to their own husbands, so that the word of God will not be dishonored."

What's the *first* item on this list of priorities? The husband! Children come later. Housework comes later. Everything else, except God, comes later. There are two very important things you can do to put your husband first and make him feel loved: play with him and pursue him sexually.

PLAY WITH HIM

In just about every survey taken of a sample of husbands—anywhere in the world—the number one thing they want from their wives is more sex. No shocker there. The number two need, however, usually comes as quite a surprise to wives: husbands wish they and their wives did more enjoyable activities together.

> *Shared activities. Shared interests. That's the heart's desire of nearly every husband.*

Your husband wants to be with you, doing something fun—a sport or a hobby. "Honey, let's play golf." "Let's go fishing." "Let's play tennis." "Let's go hunting." "Let's go to the football game, baseball game, basketball game, or NASCAR race." "Let's watch this sporting event or action-adventure movie on television." "Let's go to the mall and visit eighty-five stores, and I'll watch you touch and try on and talk about two thousand and nine articles of clothing but not actually *buy* anything."

Okay, I'm kidding about the mall. Your husband wants you to do things *he* enjoys, not necessarily what *you* enjoy. But as he works to become a more sensitive husband, he may do more activities that you find entertaining. But don't ask for that right up front. Start with *his* activities. This chapter is about his needs, not yours.

He'll love it when—at least occasionally—you join him in his leisure-time pursuits. One backdoor way to eventually get him to join you in your world, the world of talk and communication and emotional connection, is to first join him in his.

When you are doing something he likes to do, it puts him at ease. He feels relaxed. Respected. Happy. He can lower his usual male defensive guard. He's more open and may converse on a deeper level. A connection, a bridge is formed between the two of you that isn't there at any other time in your relationship. Men typically don't talk personally when they're just sitting around doing nothing. Men talk and express when they're in action or viewing something that holds their attention. If your husband is having fun with you engaging in one of his interests, he'll feel closer to you. A mood conducive to conversation is present. His tongue will be loosened, and some personal, revealing statements may slip out.

When your husband is expected to talk, and there is no fun activity going on, and you're staring at him, he has a terrible time talking. When the interesting activity is the focus and talking isn't expected, he talks. He'll say personal things to you during play times that he'd never, ever, say sitting with you in your den or at a restaurant.

You may be able to cut some deals with your husband, using your involvement in his interests as a bargaining chip. Men are basically fair-minded creatures and can understand deals. This is the "I'll scratch your back and you'll scratch mine" principle.

If he doesn't share personally during a shared activity, say to him: "Honey, I did —— [some activity] with you, and I enjoyed being with you. Now I'd like you to take me out Friday evening to a romantic restaurant and talk to me about your job, the stress you're under lately, and where we're going as a couple." Men don't like surprises, so go ahead and give him the agenda. That way he can make some notes to prepare for the meeting.

He might not go for this kind of deal. But because you met his need by spending time playing with him, he might.

PURSUE HIM SEXUALLY

If there are any men reading this far into the book, you're thinking: "Yes, yes, yes, yes, yes. Now you're talking my language."

> *Almost every husband dreams—literally dreams—that some day his wife will be more interested in sex.*

I can virtually guarantee that your husband wants more sex, and he especially wants you to be more excited about sex. He wants you to want him physically. There is nothing as invigorating and stimulating to a man as his wife wanting his body.

I have made a shocking breakthrough in my research: physical affection and sex are important to men. It is a God-given need. That's right, wives. We need sex, and if we don't get it. . .we'll die! Please, save our lives! Read the Song of Solomon, and you'll be amazed at how the Shulammite was all over Solomon. She was very attracted to his body and let him know it. Often she couldn't keep her hands off him. Solomon loved every minute of it and loved her for pursuing him physically.

Most men really like their wives to be more aggressive in the physical area. Always being the initiator gets old. Very old. Walking down the hall begging and pleading. Tugging at your skirt. "Come to me, please. Touch me. Put your hands on me. Make me feel like a man!"

Women, you know how to do this. Your husband is sitting on the couch watching television or just staring off into space. For once, there are no kids in sight. You go into the bedroom and slip into something more comfortable. You spritz on perfume: Sensuality under the Palms or You Wild Thing. You glide down the hallway in your slinky outfit, you sit down next to him and cross your legs the way you do, and then all soft and warm and sultry, you say: "Hey, big boy! New in town?"

He won't be able to shut the remote off fast enough. It's the last twenty seconds of the big game and the score is tied. He'll turn it off without a second thought. You're there, and you're looking good, and you want him.

You don't have to initiate affection and sex all the time. How about once a week or once every two weeks? Could you? Wives say to me: "Oh, I can't do this. It's embarrassing. I'm too conservative." I say, "Get over it, you prude." I'm not asking you to make advances on him in front of the neighbors or the kids. It's just you and him. Believe me, he will absolutely love it. He'll feel like a young stag. He'll feel as if he's still got it. He'll feel respected in the best possible way.

Realization:
"I felt like everything
and everybody was more
important to you than I was."—Paul

What went wrong?
- Teri's busy social life left Paul feeling unwanted.
- Paul's quiet resentment caused other tensions in the marriage.

What's going right?
- Commitment to pursue each other's interests has rejuvenated the relationship.
- The sexual relationship has recovered strongly.

Next steps:
- Continue pursuing activities together.
- Teri: Initiate sexual activity.
- Paul: Enjoy!

1. Do you have a habit of putting other persons and activities before your husband? Look at your typical day—what do you do before you give him your time and attention?

2. Ask your husband what activities he'd like you to do with him on a regular basis. Right now, schedule one of these shared activities for this week.

3. Ask your husband if he'll find it easier to talk with you during a shared activity he enjoys. Make some deals: you do something he enjoys, and he talks to you during the activity; you do something he enjoys, and the next activity is something you enjoy.

4. How much do you pursue your husband sexually? How often do you ask him for sex or unmistakably indicate that you want sex? How enthusiastic and responsive are you in bed? What is blocking you from being more aggressive in the sexual area? Pray together—right now—that God will bless and energize your sexual relationship.

Chapter 18
Marriage Makeover Achievement 15

CONFLICT CAN BE YOUR FRIEND

Put a married couple together in the same living space and you will have conflict. A lot of conflict. Disagreements involving anger and hurt feelings don't just happen in the stages of marital breakdown, but throughout the *entire life span* of the marriage. Conflict will occur with amazing frequency as long as you both shall live.

> Your Marriage Makeover will not be complete until you and your mate learn the skill of conflict resolution.

The question is not, do you have conflict? If you're both alive, you have conflict. The question is not, can you avoid conflict? Avoiding it is impossible. The question is, how do you handle your conflict?

You and your spouse have two choices: You can handle conflict poorly or well. Handling conflict poorly will inevitably lead to a dead relationship. It won't die immediately, but it will die over time, a slow, agonizing death. Every time you fail to resolve a conflict, you're a little farther apart. Eventually, you are miles apart, and no love is left.

Handling your conflict well will lead to an intimate relationship. Your disagreements create sparks and relational intensity, which, if handled correctly, produce deep emotional connection. Every time you successfully work through a conflict, the two of you will be a little closer. Each resolved conflict brings a greater knowledge of one another, which results in a greater love for one another.

> Resolved conflicts are one of the main avenues to passion.

It's easy for me to tell you to handle your conflict well. But to actually do it, you must know how. Most husbands and wives have no idea how to resolve conflict successfully. They know how not to do it, and their dysfunctional conflict pattern is killing their marriages.

Chances are very good that you resolve conflict in the same ineffective way your parents did. No one has ever taught you a step-by-step formula for successful conflict resolution. I'm going to do that right now. My formula for fair fighting isn't complicated. It's not rocket science. It's simple. But when you learn it through practice, it will work.

THE RIGHT TIME AND PLACE
When conflict first hits, and words expressing anger are just starting to come out of your mouth, you must call an immediate cease-fire, and each of you must go to a

neutral corner. You say, "But we haven't even begun to talk about it yet!" I reply, "Exactly. When anger initially hits, no one is ready to talk about it."

Many couples make the mistake of trying to talk about a conflict too quickly. Sandy and I made this mistake for years until we figured out it was a disaster and that it just made our conflicts worse.

When a conflict surfaces, you are not ready to deal with it yet. Tempers are high. The level of emotional intensity is at its peak. You're running on adrenaline. You're fueled by the "fight or flight" syndrome. You're not thinking clearly, and your mouth will go into over-drive. Both of you will say things you don't mean, and damage will be done. And, of course, the conflict has no chance of being resolved. "The tongue is a small part of the body, and yet it boasts of great things. See how great a forest is set aflame by such a small fire! And the tongue is a fire, the very world of iniquity" (James 3:5–6).

Sound familiar? How many times have you acted out this verse in a conflict? Yeah, me, too. This is not what you want as your life verse.

It's natural to want to launch immediately into a con-flict and go back and forth over the issue. When you've been stung, your mouth is triggered, and you want to sting back to "clarify the issue" and state your case—right now. There is usually one partner who wants to talk it out right away and get it resolved. No. Don't do it. It's a bad idea. Here's the wisdom of Solomon: "The beginning of strife is like letting out water, so abandon the quarrel before it breaks out" (Proverbs 17:14).

Here's what I want you to do when a conflict begins. Tell your partner, "I'm angry, we have a problem to deal with, and I'll let you know when I'm ready to discuss it." Then skedaddle away from your partner and the scene of the potential crime. You need to get space as soon as possible. The less talking in this first phase of conflict resolution, the better. Again in Proverbs we read, "There is one who speaks rashly like the thrusts of a sword" (12:18). Don't even attempt to schedule the time and place for the discussion. That's too much talking, and there's a huge risk of saying something you'll regret.

Each of you needs to go to a private place to cool down and pray for God's help to deal with the conflict. Even a few minutes will help you calm down from your peak of emotional intensity. You may still be angry and hurt but not furious and in full battle mode.

When you have simmered down and feel prepared to begin the discussion of the conflict, go to your partner (or call on the telephone) and say, "I'm ready to talk now. Let me know when you're ready." When your spouse indicates readiness, schedule the time and place for the conflict discussion.

The time ought to be as soon as possible. Ephesians 4:26–27 says, "Be angry and yet do not sin; do not let the sun go down on your anger, and do not give the devil an opportunity." You probably won't get all the way through the conflict on the first day, but God clearly wants your anger to be expressed and released in a harmless, non-threatening way—"speaking the truth in love" (Ephesians 4:15)—before the end of the first day.

The place should be a location in your home that is private, quiet, and neutral. The children should not overhear your discussion. This doesn't mean that you hide from them the truth that Mom and Dad have disagreements and disputes, but that you resolve them. By neutral, I mean not warm and cozy and intimate. Don't use your bedroom or the special place you use for couple times. I usually recommend the kitchen or dining room table. When you choose a conflict place, agree that this will be the location you will use to discuss most of your conflicts. It helps to limit and contain your conflict resolutions to one spot. It provides structure and control.

Obviously, if you're out of town, you won't be able to use this location, and you will have to use the phone for the first part of the conflict discussion.

ONE AT A TIME

When you are seated in your conflict location, sufficiently cooled down and individually "prayed up," pray out loud for God's help to work through the conflict. I prefer that both spouses pray briefly, but if only one will pray, I strongly recommend it be the husband. Spiritual leadership. Enough said.

After a short prayer, one spouse will go first and share

his or her feelings, thoughts, and point of view about the disagreement. This spouse is the *Speaker*, which makes the other spouse the *Listener*. For this stage and the next stage of the conflict resolution process, you will stay rigidly attached to these Speaker-Listener roles.

Communication will be one at a time. There must be one Speaker and one Listener at all times, with no interchange or interruptions. If both spouses speak, there is no understanding and therefore no resolution. If both spouses speak, the two tongues take over, and the result is chaos and raised voices and nasty comments and a big, fat, ugly mess.

The Speaker, in ten minutes or less, says what he or she needs to say about the issue. The Speaker shares his or her opinion, feelings, and position. The Listener may disagree, but what the Speaker says can't be wrong; it is the Speaker's truth. To oppose it is saying, "You can't feel that way! I deny you the right to feel that way or have your beliefs about it."

The Listener's job is to say nothing original, but rather to help the Speaker feel understood. The Listener achieves this understanding and clearly shows this to his or her spouse by being an *active listener* (see chapter 8), which means reflecting back what the Speaker is saying and the feelings being expressed. To be true to what the Speaker has said, the Listener should use the Speaker's words rather than his or her own.

In other words, the Listener stuffs his or her feelings

and point of view for the moment and focuses on the Speaker's message and making sure the Speaker feels understood.

The Listener says things like: "You're saying that my comment about your sister made you feel angry and hurt." "You wonder if I've ever liked your sister." "You're deeply offended because you love your sister and feel close to her." "It's important to you that I respect your family and at least get along with your sister. Is that right?"

You don't move on until the Speaker confirms that the Listener understands. Although the Speaker's opening statement has a ten-minute limit (it is often a good idea to set a timer), it may take longer to achieve understanding. Take the time needed to clarify the Speaker's message, because this first link of understanding is critical. Without a connection here, resolution has no chance of happening.

Keep in mind that I'm talking about *understanding*, not *agreement*. You're going to disagree, that's why they call it a conflict. Besides, you're a man and a woman. You disagree on a lot of things anyway. There will always be two points of view and two sets of feelings in every conflict. *You both are right.* What we are doing is working for both of you to get understanding of your respective truths.

When understanding has been reached because the one who is the Speaker at the time says so, it's time for a break. Let the achieved understanding rest for a while so that it truly takes hold. If the Listener takes his or her turn too soon, cranks up right away, and begins sharing his or her truth, the delicate, newborn understanding of the Speaker's truth easily can be wiped out.

So leave your seats for a bit—ten minutes at a minimum. It might be half an hour, one hour, or even two hours. I prefer a short time if it's possible. Remember, you are dealing essentially with one issue, not all the complaints or disagreements or bad feelings of the past ten years. If the Listener is really struggling with anger and other intense emotions, or wrestling with the Speaker's message, it will take longer to settle before the Listener takes his or her turn as Speaker.

After the break, return to your seats and reverse roles. The Listener is now the Speaker, and vice versa. The new Speaker will share his or her feelings, opinions, and point of view about the same issue introduced by the first Speaker. The new Speaker will now present a second truth, which is as equally valid as the first, and it is the new Listener's job to reflect and build understanding. Follow the same process as with the first Speaker, allowing the new Speaker up to ten minutes to state his or her case.

The truth expressed by the second Speaker may be totally different from what the first Speaker said. It may represent a totally different point of view and set of emotions. No one is lying. As you would expect, a different person of a different gender is going to express a different truth.

Take the time necessary to build this second bridge of understanding. Don't move on until the new Speaker feels understood and says so. You don't have to agree. This is a good thing, because you won't. You can't! Regardless of the issue, you will see it and feel it your way. Same for your partner. But you can and must work to understand and fully accept and validate your partner's feelings and point of view.

PROCESSING

When the two truths have been expressed, and both spouses feel understood, it's time for another break. Let the two understandings resonate and settle in for a while. The good news is that, at this point, you are three-quarters of the way to resolution. The bad news is that you're not done yet, and it's easy to mess it up unless you follow the guidelines.

Your break may last just ten minutes, or it may last until the next day. If you're getting the impression that conflict requires time to resolve, you're right. Slow and steady is the way to successful resolution. You'll need this break to think about what has already happened and mull it over in your heart and mind. The anger is out and largely released, so you've obeyed Ephesians 4:26–27. But you need to let your brains rest and process the issues that have been discussed.

When you're ready to continue the conflict discussion, let your partner know. When your partner signals readiness, schedule a time to resume talking in your conflict-resolution location.

When you get back to it, you will still take turns as Speaker and Listener. I call this the Processing stage because you will review the topics and emotions already shared in an attempt to solidify understanding and emotional connection. You will work for clarification. You will do more venting of emotions, if necessary, but *not ever* to hurt or punish your mate. You will seek reassurance that your spouse really does understand you.

The wife, because she is a woman, especially needs this Processing stage. A woman typically has to go over an issue several times before she can release it. She processes more than a man will and does it out loud more than he does. That's okay. She needs to do it, so let her do it without any hesitancy or impatience on the part of the husband. She needs to fully express herself and be confident that her ideas and feelings are fully understood.

If, at the end of the Processing stage, you have talked out your truths until you both feel understood and reconnected, and if there is no decision to be made, you're done! But if your conflict requires a decision of some kind, you will move on to the Let's Make a Deal stage.

LET'S MAKE A DEAL

Before you start the Let's Make a Deal stage, guess what you're going to do? That's right—take another break. This break should be for a few minutes to half a day or more. When both partners are ready to resume, agree on a time and return one more time to your conflict-resolution location.

If you must decide on some course of action or some behavior—a financial move, a parenting strategy, a schedule change, or something you want your partner to do or not do—you will need to work together to make a deal. With most of the anger gone and a substantial amount of understanding achieved, you will be in good shape to negotiate and reach an agreement. It is usually okay to go back and forth in this stage without staying in the Speaker-Listener roles. But if things begin to get too intense, go right back to those roles.

Pray again as you enter this decision stage. God will help you hammer out a deal. Agree on specific behaviors that can be measured. Avoid vague decisions like, "Let's see if we can do better." What does such a statement mean? Nobody knows.

Here's an example of a good, tight, specific deal:

Wife: "I'd be happy if you would at least call me before 5:00 p.m. every workday and tell me when you expect to get home. Even if you're late, it will help me to know in advance."

Husband: "Okay. I'll call you each day before 5:00 p.m. and let you know when I expect to get home."

> Be willing to compromise. You won't get your way every time.
> Sometimes you'll get your way; and sometimes your spouse
> will get his or hers. Sometimes you'll meet in the middle with
> a deal that includes ideas from both of you.

Every deal is on a trial basis. If it doesn't work, call a meeting and go back to the table and renegotiate. Don't make a deal you don't like. Stay at this renegotiation until you reach a decision you both can live with.

TAKE IT SLOWLY

It will take a minimum of two days to work through the vast majority of your conflicts. Do not expect to get through in one sitting. Unless it's an extremely minor conflict, it simply can't be done. You can get your anger out by the end of the first day, but the whole process takes time. It will take five, six, or seven sit-down talks over two, three, or even four days to successfully resolve a conflict. More intense, nastier conflicts could easily take a week or more.

It's important to nurture your relationship in other areas as you work your way through a conflict. Talk about other subjects in your regular couple times, meet needs, make love, and be affectionate. A conflict doesn't need to grind your relationship, the pleasure of being together, to a halt, especially after the initial anger is released and dissipates. You can develop the skill of maintaining a positive flow as a couple while the conflict-resolution process is running its course.

STOP AND START

When a conflict conversation gets off track, even slightly, shut it down immediately. Don't try to save it by trying to get back to a good place. You can't do that. No couple can. That conversation is over. Take a time-out right away, and leave your conflict location. Either spouse can call for a stop, and it must be honored. It might be just five minutes. When you're ready to resume, tell your partner and ask him or her to find you when ready. Then sit down again and start back up where you left off.

If the husband raises his voice, stop, take a break, and start again. If the wife talks way beyond her ten-minute limit, and the husband is getting frustrated and overwhelmed, stop, take a break, and restart. If the wife shuts down and clams up, stop, take a break, and restart. If the husband won't honor a break and follows his wife down the hall talking, stop, take a break, and restart. If one spouse doesn't stick to the issue and brings up other issues, stop, take a break, and restart. Any violation of the Speaker-Listener rule should also trigger a stop, break, restart.

No matter what happens to disturb the operation of the conflict-resolution formula, you need to stop and restart. As you learn how to follow these steps, you'll stop and start frequently. That's acceptable. It's healthy and normal and a lot better than chewing on each other and going back to your old way of fighting.

IF YOUR SPOUSE WON'T COOPERATE
If your spouse refuses to work with you in following this formula for resolving conflicts, you'll have no choice

but to use the one-way communication technique I explained in chapter 11.

When you're angry and hurt, go and express yourself briefly to your spouse. Share what's on your heart, ask for a response when he or she is ready, and walk away. This keeps your system clean, and you'll be able to forgive regardless of your spouse's reaction. If your spouse does not respond, go back and express your feelings about that. Then drop it and move on. If your spouse won't even listen to your one-way verbal communications, write him or her notes.

Will you lose respect for your spouse if he or she refuses to join you in a healthy conflict resolution process? Yes. Will you lose love? Yes. Will you be forced to pull back emotionally and physically to protect yourself and the relationship? Yes. All you can do is regularly tell your spouse about these consequences in the one-way fashion, and ask for God's help and strength to continue to be the spouse that God wants you to be, despite the circumstances.

SNAPSHOT
AMY AND MIKE

Realization:
"Our conflicts were killing our marriage."
—Amy

What went wrong?
- Old conflict patterns were doing much relationship damage.
- Amy would get emotional; Mike would shut down.
- Amy would become even angrier with Mike's silence.

What's going right?
- The "stop and start" process is helping resolve conflict.
- Hurt and anger are being brought into the open for resolution.

Next steps:
- Continue to use conflict resolution tools to strengthen the marriage.
- Enjoy the fruits of a healthier marriage.

1. How much conflict do you and your spouse experience? How many conflicts do you usually have in a week? In a month?
2. What do you typically fight about? What are the top three or four conflicts—the ones you fight about over and over?
3. How do you fight? What pattern do you follow when there's a conflict? What does your husband do? What does your wife do? How does not resolving conflicts negatively affect your marriage?
4. Do you think that meeting the other fourteen Marriage Makeover Achievements will help reduce the number of your conflicts? Which specific needs, if met, would cause you to have less conflict?
5. Pick a recent conflict, something small and not too intense, and practice working through it using my fair fighting formula that I've described in this chapter.

Chapter 19

IT'S TIME FOR ACTION

This may be the shortest final chapter of any marriage book ever written. Maybe I'll get into *Guinness World Records*.

There isn't much more to write. I've described the five types of marriages. I've told you it's going to be tough to change. I've promised you that you can change your present marriage into a great marriage. I've explained in very practical terms the fifteen Marriage Makeover Achievements.

The Marriage Makeover program works. I've seen God use it to transform hundreds of marriages. God used it to transform my marriage. It's rooted in Scripture and the needs that God says are most critical in the lives of husbands and wives. God will use this makeover process to transform your marriage, too. *You just have to do it.* A certain shoe and apparel company was not the first to coin the phrase "Just do it!" God, through His servant, James, was the first: "Prove yourselves doers of the word, and not merely hearers who delude themselves" (James

1:22). It's time to start your Marriage Makeover. So just do it. With your spouse, go back and reread each chapter. Use your couple times to discuss what you've read, and follow the Makeover Steps.

Don't just talk about it. Don't let your lame excuses get in the way. Don't stall. Don't let anything or anyone stop you. Do it. Do it now.

You can stay in your marriage as it is now, or you can build a fulfilling, passionate, intimate, one-flesh, Genesis 2:24, Ephesians 5:31 marriage. The marriage you've always wanted. The marriage God has always wanted for you. It's up to you.

OTHER BOOKS BY DAVID CLARKE

Men Are Clams, Women Are Crowbars

A Marriage after God's Own Heart

What to Do When Your Spouse Says,
"I Don't Love You Anymore"

*****

To schedule a seminar or order Dr. Clarke's
books, videotapes, and DVDs, please
contact:
DAVID CLARKE SEMINARS
www.davidclarkeseminars.com
1-888-516-8844
or
Marriage & Family Enrichment Center
6505 North Himes Avenue
Tampa, FL 33614